My Life as a
FURRY RED
MONSTER

What Being Elmo Has Taught Me
About Life, Love,
and Laughing Out Loud

KEVIN CLASH

with Gary Brozek

Illustrations by Louis Henry Mitchell

Broadway Books
New York

PUBLISHED BY BROADWAY BOOKS

Published in the United States by Broadway Books, an imprint of The Doubleday
Broadway Publishing Group, a division of Random House, Inc., New York.

www.broadwaybooks.com

BROADWAY BOOKS and its logo, a letter B bisected on the diagonal,
are trademarks of Random House, Inc.

Book design by Chris Welch

Library of Congress Cataloging-in-Publication Data
Clash, Kevin.
My life as a furry red monster : what being Elmo has taught me about life,
love, and laughing out loud / Kevin Clash with Gary Brozek.—1st ed.
p. cm.
1. Clash, Kevin. 2. Puppeteers—United States—Biography.
I. Brozek, Gary. II. Title.
PN1982.C53A3 2006
791.5'3092—dc22
[B]
2006047592

ISBN-13: 978-0-7679-2375-0
ISBN-10: 0-7679-2375-8

PRINTED IN THE UNITED STATES OF AMERICA

1   3   5   7   9   10   8   6   4   2

First Edition

TO MOM AND DAD,
FOR ALL THE CARING, LOVE, AND SUPPORT

CONTENTS

My Life as a

FURRY RED
MONSTER

WELCOME TO "ELMO'S WORLD"— AND MY WORLD, TOO

*O*nce upon a time, a young man was given a special but unusual set of gifts: a fuzzy mop of cherry-red fur, crowned with two enormous eyes, which sat high atop an orange egg of a nose that resembled, well, an orange egg. The young man seemed to know exactly what to do with his gifts, as you will soon see, but he added one more thing to the mix: a high-pitched voice brimming with joy, and a laugh like no other that would capture, soothe, and delight the hearts of millions both young and old. Yet like Jack's magic beans, Dorothy's ruby slippers, and Frodo's golden ring, the full power of these gifts wouldn't be revealed to their owner until later in the story . . .

Like many a fairy tale, mine begins a long time ago in a faraway land, called New York City.

"Give it a voice, Clash," challenged Richard Hunt, a master Muppeteer and my *Sesame Street* colleague, tossing me a shapeless, soft bundle of red that I caught in midair. Back then I was still a very junior employee, wondering how much longer my dream job as a Muppeteer-in-training would last. Some days, as I worked away at playing chickens and pigs and AMs (Anything Muppets), clucking and oinking (and barking, squeaking, or hooting) my way through the television studio in New York, I remembered that I was only a train ride away from Turner's Station, Maryland, my hometown on the Chesapeake Bay where I happily and unwittingly took the first steps on a path that would lead me right here, to West Fifty-ninth Street.

Without thinking, I grabbed the little monster and put him high on my arm, all at once letting loose with a boundless, childlike laugh—a falsetto squeal that would change my life. "Hello, it's Elmo!" called this creature in the happiest of voices. "Hi, everybody!"

Now the adrenaline surged through me, as if a magic wand had been waved, and suddenly I wasn't in New York. In a flash, I was a kid again back home in Turner's Station, with a blanket strung over the clothesline for a makeshift stage, doing a puppet show for my mom's daycare kids, lip-synching Earth, Wind & Fire songs. "Another one, another one!" they'd beg, wanting the show to go on. Back then, I had a captive audience. But now, my audience could just change the channel. There was more at stake than my youthful ego—I was working for Jim Henson now, and on one of the most prestigious and popular television shows for children ever created.

But on that day back in 1983, when I greeted Richard as a three-

and-a-half-year-old little monster who seemingly came out of nowhere, I wasn't thinking about that grown-up stuff. Instead, I was soaking up the magic of inspiration, remembering the pure and simple fun of being a child, and claiming the gift that had literally been thrown at me.

Elmo was born.

MY LIFE AS A FUZZY RED MONSTER is a real-life fairy tale, complete with a rise from obscurity to fame, some wonderful fairy godmothers and godfathers, a villain or two, a cast of loyal townspeople, some pitfalls, and more than a few morals. I started out as a kid who loved to draw and build things, whose imagination was fired not only by the fun-loving family surrounding me, but by the countless hours I spent in front of the television, watching everything from *Captain Kangaroo* to *Jonny Quest*, from *All in the Family* and *Good Times* to *The Mike Douglas Show*, and, of course, *Sesame Street*.

Gradually I overcame my youthful shyness by performing puppet shows first for neighborhood kids, then all around the Baltimore area, at schools, churches, community events, and later on local television shows. I had always dared to dream large, but even this black kid's imagination could not have come close to inventing the storybook success that I have enjoyed in the nearly thirty years I've worked in this medium I adore.

This is my story, but it's also Elmo's. Elmo connects with people on a level beyond any other character I've performed, and I think I know why. Though he represents youthful curiosity and innocence, behind his childlike simplicity you'll find the wisdom of an old soul, an unfailing sense of humor (and the laugh to go with it), and a loving, lovable hero with a heart worthy of any fairy tale. You'll also discover, as I have, that Elmo is a teacher whose lessons can have a lasting value for adults, not just for the countless children he reaches each day.

What most of us envy about kids is the simplicity of their early years, when having a close family, friends to play with, and unlimited new worlds to discover are the only ingredients needed for a happy life. We long for those days when we would speak our minds and do our thing without worrying about the consequences, mostly oblivious to the past and the future. Children, after all, are masters at the art of living in the moment. And so is Elmo. (It turns out that getting to be three and a half all your life is a pretty good gig!)

As adults, we can't return to those simple days of childhood, but we can draw on their lessons to recapture some very basic pleasures, like that joyful feeling that the sky's the limit. If you are a parent, as I am, you've witnessed a certain no-holds-barred spirit in your youngster and undoubtedly you've looked for ways to nurture that quality, to help your child discover and follow his passions.

That type of nurturing is one of the things that Elmo does best (and my own parents did an excellent job of it, as well), but it doesn't have to end once a little girl or boy no longer watches *Sesame Street*. True, sooner or later, he'll trade up from crayons to computer keyboards, or she'll exchange imaginary friends for trips to the mall with real friends, but there is a certain magical quality of childhood that can be preserved and used as an inner strength throughout adulthood.

Being Elmo helps me tap in to those lessons of childhood every single day of my adult life, and now I want to share what I've learned—about love, joy, creativity, friendship, and so much more—with you. I believe that this little red monster may hold the key to unlocking that most elusive of fairy-tale treasures: a happy life with promise of a happy ending.

1

LOVE

WHEN I TELL folks what I do for a living *("What'dya mean you're Elmo? You're a forty-five-year-old six-foot African American male with a deep voice, get outta here")*, after they regain their composure, they ask me to explain Elmo's popularity. Elmo is instantly recognizable in nearly every country in the world. He knows heads of state, A-list celebrities, world-class athletes, Oscar winners, Tony winners, Grammy winners, spelling-bee winners, and lots of babies. If Elmo had a cell phone, it would never stop ringing. Why is this little fur-and-foam bundle of energy such a phenomenon?

I have a one-word answer: love. Elmo connects with children and adults on the purest and most fundamental level, and that is the human desire to love and be loved. It's as simple as that.

Though I've said "Elmo loves you" thousands of times, maybe

millions, the thrill remains because children crave hearing that they are loved. (So do most adults, even if they won't admit it.) And kids love to say it back—"I love you, too!"—and you know they mean it, no matter how many times they say it.

"I love you." Those are magic words—basic, simple, easy to say, but as adults we often forget their power. We often forget to say them. But Elmo reminds me on a daily basis that love is the foundation for a happy life. And before we can love each other, we have to learn to love ourselves.

BACK HOME IN Turner's Station, a blue-collar community located just east of downtown Baltimore, Maryland, there was plenty of love to go around. In fact, my mom had so much love to give that she shared it with all the neighbor kids, running a family-style daycare center out of our two-bedroom, one-bath home. My siblings—Georgie (the oldest, George Jr.), big sister Anita (we called her Ne-Ne), and little sister Pam—grew up in a kind of kid heaven, where children and love naturally intersected and were never in short supply.

Money, however, was. Officially, my hometown is called Turner Station, but we always referred to it as Turner's Station—just tradition among the locals, I guess. It's fitting that the name confusion exists, because there really are two towns in my mind—the Turner's Station of my youth and memory and the Turner Station of a harsher reality. My father worked hard as a flash welder operator at Raymond Metals to put a roof over our heads, and Mom's daycare work supplemented his income. But that said, I never, ever felt poor in that house, though there were days when all we had for dinner were mayonnaise sandwiches.

Our small brick ranch house on New Pittsburgh Avenue was an unremarkable structure, not much different (at least on the outside) from most others in the neighborhood. It had a side entry and a two-step cement stoop where the neighborhood men often sat smoking and chatting in the quiet of a summer's evening. A chain-link fence kept the constant flow of bicycle, tricycle, wagon, hopscotch, and jump-rope traffic off our small patch of lawn and out of the few geraniums, petunias, and four-o'clocks my mother tried to keep thriving in her front-yard garden.

If our property was remarkable in any way, it was because we had two sheds in the backyard instead of the usual one. My father was, and is, an inveterate pack rat. His excuse was that in addition to his day job, he brought in money by being a neighborhood handyman. So any scrap he could salvage from a demolition or remodeling job went into the bursting-at-the-seams shed.

"You can't believe what someone threw away today," he'd announce at dinner, recounting his latest find. Before long, like my dad, I started saving and salvaging my own scraps—old buttons, fabric, a worn-out fuzzy slipper, odd bits of plastic or Styrofoam, boxes—any materials that I could turn into the simple puppets I began building and fiddling with as a child.

Now, lest you start picturing a *Sanford and Son* type of junk lot—

even though Dad was often told that he looked like Redd Foxx—you need to know that our house sat just a few hundred yards from the Chesapeake Bay. We had a huge backyard dominated by a willow tree, and beyond our lawn a field of tall fescue grass waved in the warm breezes off the water. Depending on the wind direction and tide, the air was filled with the sweet scent of the salty water or the fertile smell of the tacky mudflats we delighted stomping through in search of seashells. On the worst days, the chemical odors from the nearby Bethlehem Steel mill at Sparrows Point overpowered all.

We lived within a half hour ride of vibrant downtown Baltimore, yet our neighborhood was a bucolic mix of homes and vacant fields where we roamed and aired our young imaginations. Necessity remained the true mother of invention, however, and we kids weren't the only creative ones. I still remember one field where enterprising Mr. Shelton parked a school bus he had converted into a general store. Mom would send me to this mobile pit stop for a few necessities, saving her a trip to Miss Hill's grocery farther away on Wade Street.

My mom was the ultimate "working mother," before that phrase came into vogue. Not only was she busy raising my siblings and me, she had a house full of neighborhood kids in the daycare center she ran. As a result, growing up, my home was filled with the controlled (and sometimes uncontrolled) chaos that children bring. With the four of us there, plus the half dozen or so kids from the neighborhood Mom watched, all that energy exerted a magnetic pull on other toddlers and preteens in the neighborhood.

Our house was a place where many kids took their first staggering steps, where the smell of baby powder and dirty diapers dueled for dominance, and where each evening my mother leaned her hip wearily against the counter as she prepared dinner, while I sat at the table making art with assorted empty cereal and Kleenex boxes, colored paper, crayons, and Elmer's glue. I kept one eye on my creation-in-progress and the other on the paper towel roll, waiting for that last sheet to be torn off so I could pounce on the cardboard cylinder and claim it.

I undoubtedly inherited my "crafty" instincts from my parents, Gladys and George Clash. Mom sewed like a pro, and Dad loved to draw and make things, and they often got into the spirit of creating with us kids. Once, after a huge snowstorm, my parents helped us construct a massive snow fort—a squared-off igloo. Mom made a flag for us to fly using iron-on letters on red cloth. Though the snow melted, the name we gave to our winter playhouse stuck, and the red flag found a place in our living room. From that point forward my house was known as Fort McKids.

Between neighborhood children, my many relatives who lived nearby, the daycare kids and their parents constantly dropping by, our home life was structured mayhem. And as on *Sesame Street*, humor was a mainstay. I'm grateful for having grown up in what was basically "kid central," because it later made being on the set of *Sesame Street* feel like I was back with my family. With that many kids around, you can be sure that on any given day, the house was populated by at least one grouch and several monsters, and a cookie was certainly something to be devoured, not savored or shared.

Though our house was modest, my sense of home felt larger than our four walls. It extended into the multitude of other homes in which I felt welcome. As a kid, I loved the *Sesame Street* song, "People in Your Neighborhood," because it perfectly captured the connectedness I felt in mine. The homes of our neighbors, Mr. Bernard and his wife, Miss Rose, and Mr. Melvin and Miss Lee, as well as Miss Ada, Miss Marie, and Miss Eunice, were nearly as familiar as my own. I can still taste the crabs my father's friend Kakie (never Mr. Kakie, always just Kakie) shared with us.

No matter how much activity was going on in the house, I always carved out time to watch *Sesame Street* and other children's shows. My mother never used television as an electronic babysitter, but I'm like so many of my generation with a fierce devotion to the medium that came into our homes on a small screen and somehow enlarged our world beyond all measure.

Sesame Street first aired when I was ten years old, and as soon as I heard the sprightly opening bars of the theme song, I was entranced. I was one of those up-close sitters. I'd park myself a few inches from the RCA color television set we had. I was so close, I could feel the static electricity of the screen tugging at the peach fuzz on my face and smell the wonderful aroma of electrically heated dust coming from the vents of that lustrous wooden console. No matter how many times my mother yelled, "Kevin! Move back before you go blind!" I'd still feel myself powerfully drawn into that world, and the worn-out seats of my Lee jeans bore witness to the pull I was powerless to resist.

I was instantly taken with this new show, with these creatures called "Muppets"—Jim Henson's trademark way of combining "marionette" and "puppet"—and little did I know that I was already setting the course of my life to exchange my New Pittsburgh Avenue address for 123 Sesame Street. Love makes you do crazy things sometimes.

HE MAY NOT look like it, but that Elmo's a love machine.

When parents tell me, "My child lives for Elmo," I tell them that Elmo lives because of their child's love for him. I don't just mean that Elmo is alive in their child's imagination, though that is certainly a part of it. That child and Elmo aren't just experiencing love; they're creating more of it to go around, and in doing so they make the world a better place.

It works like this: Elmo feeds off the love he receives from kids, from the adult characters on the show, and from his fellow Muppets. He doesn't just take that love in as a fuel and use it up. Instead, he drinks it in and gives it right back in spades. He's a kind of love-energy power station, and the more love he takes in, the more love he produces for the rest of the world. The more love he produces, the more love he receives, and the cycle completes itself over and over again. Talk about a renewable resource!

I first saw this powerful cycle in action shortly after Elmo debuted and was gaining in popularity in the mid-1980s, when I did an appearance with him at a school in the Bronx. A group of preschoolers were gathered in the library, all of them bundles of fidgeting energy with their legs swinging like metronomes. As soon as Elmo said, "Hello, everybody! Elmo loves you!" it was like a floodgate had opened, and Elmo and I were awash in a surge of little children. I could almost feel an electric charge in the room, as their shouts of "I love you, Elmo!" reverberated off the cinder-block walls. Elmo laughed and opened his arms wide and tried to scoop up all the love and hug it to his chest, all the while repeating "Elmo loves you, too."

That may have been the first time in my adult life when I finally comprehended the ancient notion that what you put out in the universe comes back to you. Since that day, I've learned to try to put as much Elmo and Kevin love out into the world as I can, knowing that it will have a very positive ripple effect. Elmo and the children taught me that one. Somewhere along the road to adulthood, we seem to forget this little secret about the power of love, but it's worth remembering.

When children tell Elmo that they love him, they all have different styles of expressing their emotion. Some of the more demonstrative kids throw their arms around his neck, snuggle their faces against his, and with an eyes-closed, sigh-heaving, hand-me-my-Tony-Award gesture that projects to the very last row of the theater's balcony, they proclaim their undying devotion to Elmo in prose as purple as

Telly Monster. "Oh, Elmo, I love you more than chocolate ice cream! More than I love the new baby! Please come and live in my house forever!"

Older kids are a little more matter-of-fact, as if they've been married for twenty years and they're picking up their keys and their bag and heading out the door with an affectionate but perfunctory "Love you." Still others are more shy and reserved, like the bashful and nervous teen letting his or her feelings be known to their crush for the first time. I often wonder how these children will express their love as adults and how many of them will remain demonstrative and unembarrassed, or if they'll naturally pull back into more conservative styles as they grow older. It would be ridiculous if we all greeted each other the way the more enthusiastic kids greet Elmo—imagine how long it would take to get that first cup of coffee at the office with all the morning greetings in full swing!—but still, doesn't imagining a love-filled world like that put a smile on your face?

Children approach Elmo differently depending on their age, but they also are inevitably influenced by the kinds of physical demonstrations of affection they receive at home. Elmo wants to reach all kids, and sometimes he can be like that overly enthusiastic puppy who finds everything in the world so fresh and new and wonderful that he can't contain himself. Just as kids may squeal in delight when they first see a puppy and then retreat in leg-hugging, face-shielding fear when the puppy starts to jump on them, Elmo can evoke the same response. Over time, I've learned to think quickly on my feet, to gauge the kinds of responses I'm getting from a child and either tone down or amp up Elmo's enthusiasm level accordingly. I constantly have to remind myself that even though they've seen Elmo countless times on television, they're meeting him face-to-face for the very first time.

The funny thing is, no two kids are alike. I've seen the quiet ones respond with smiles and giggles that escalate to a full-on Elmo love attack—the eardrum-piercing, vibrating, arms-wide, hugging and squeezing and kissing frontal assault. Other shy kids need a little bit of time to warm up to Elmo and his "de-monster-ative" displays of affection. But in the end, they all come around.

If only we adults could just remember to let our hearts do the talking sometimes, like kids do. Back in December of 2001, we held the first and only MuppetFest in Santa Monica. This was a weekend event for the general public and for television industry insiders. Along with projecting clips of the shows on giant screens and discussing the history of the Muppets, Jim Henson's London Based Creature Shop (where they built puppets used in films such as *Teenage Mutant Ninja Turtles* and animatronic creatures like those in *Babe*) held seminars on the making and maintenance of the puppets, the use of computer-generated images in children's television, advances in electronics and radio-controlled puppetry, and a host of other topics. As performers, we didn't attend every seminar, but we did all gather for the question-and-answer session. We sat on stage at the Civic Auditorium, each of us with a puppet on our arms.

Now, this wasn't a gathering of kids; the audience was a collection of adults who grew up watching the show, a number of them dressed in full walk-around costumes of their favorite Muppet, and I noticed more than one super-size Elmo. These folks made me realize the connection between the words "fan" and "fanatic." (Okay, it was a little like a Trekkie convention.) Most of all, the stuff they knew—from behind-the-scenes trivia to highly technical details—blew me away. The questions ranged widely, and we talked about everything from diversity among the cast and characters and the future of the Muppets, to new directions the *Sesame Street* curriculum might take. It was great to have such an intelligent and passionate audience, and we tried to have fun with it all, but then something happened to put the whole thing into perspective and to remind us why we were up there in the first place.

We'd placed a microphone in each aisle, where people lined up to ask their questions. At one point, I noticed a stirring in the audience, and I saw a little African American girl walking down the aisle. I thought maybe she'd gotten up to stand beside her mommy or something like that. I kept an eye on her. She didn't stop by anyone in line; she just kept coming. We were on a raised stage, and when she got right up to the edge of it, she rested her elbows on the stage floor and cupped her chin on her hands, staring straight in my direction. But she wasn't looking at Kevin Clash. "Hi, Elmo!" she piped.

Steve Whitmire was fielding a question about the responsibility he felt in taking over as Kermit after Jim Henson died, so I don't think too many people heard her. I did, but I didn't want to interrupt Steve's response.

"Hi, Elmo," she repeated. "I love you."

This time her voice was louder. I couldn't let Elmo ignore her, so I had him wave, but I knew that wouldn't hold her. I was dying to get Elmo over to her. By this time, the folks in the front rows who'd seen and heard her started murmuring, and Steve and everyone else onstage were looking at the little girl. I went to the edge of the stage. Elmo bent over and hugged her and said, "Hello. Elmo loves you, too." He put his arms around her and hugged and kissed her. That girl's smile lit up the entire darkened portion of the auditorium. She hugged him back and they said their good-byes before she gleefully ran back to her mother.

The audience burst into applause. This little girl could not come to an event where her friend was and not say hello to him. She had to connect with him and tell him that she loved him. All the rest, the reminiscences and the revelations about new developments, didn't matter to her. After that exchange with the child, that stuff seemed to matter a little less to those of us onstage and in the audience, too. That's the power of giving and receiving love.

MANY OF THE qualities that I observed in my mother as she interacted with her daycare kids are ones I use in puppeteering: having eyes in the back of your head, split-second instincts, improvising, taking genuine delight in the fresh point of view of children and the amazing insights they have, and remaining positive amid mayhem—including trying (and ultimately failing) not to laugh when disciplining a misbehaving child. Those are all wonderful skills, but they are things that you *do*. What separates my mother is more than the sum of what she can do; it is who she *is*, some essence she possesses and broadcasts, not via UHF, VHF, cable, satellite, or Internet, but person to person, soul to soul. I've tried to emulate my mother, and as a result, Elmo possesses and shares with the world that same broadcast-quality love.

To be a truly successful puppeteer, to not only entertain but really connect with children, I must reach into my own heart to project love to every boy and girl in the audience—even when I can't see them. My mother set a powerful example for me by loving all her daycare children as if they were her flesh and blood. When I am performing Elmo in front of the camera, I remind myself that somewhere out there, there's an impressionable kid perched as close to the television as I used to sit, feeling that same electromagnetic pull, wanting to reach through that screen to touch and be touched. Like my mother, like Elmo, I strive to touch the heart of every child I come into contact with, because that connection is so vital.

From time to time, my mother encountered children who needed extra love and understanding. These weren't the kids who would draw on the couch with crayons. (Those I prefer to think of as "creative risk takers"—little puppeteers-in-the-making whom I identified with.) If my mother saw a child who needed a supplement to the love and attention they got at home, she would become their advocate on every level. She gave love generously, just the way Elmo does. One child, a shy, sensitive little girl with few friends who was often picked on at school, told my mother sadly, "Miss Gladys, those other kids don't ever want to sit by me."

Her words set my mother in motion. Mom made sure the girl's mother knew how her daughter was feeling and began to build up the child's confidence by telling her over and over that she was intelligent and talented. She defended her against neighborhood bullies, and she even wrote a letter to the child's teacher asking her to be on the alert for other kids who were teasing her.

Slowly but surely, the other kids did want to play with the child. My mother gave this little girl love like she was one of her own, and the result was a child who blossomed. Love was my mother's weapon of choice, and it worked every time. Many years later, as an adult, that girl returned to Turner's Station, and she thanked my mother for all she'd done to build up her self-esteem and make her feel valued. And she wasn't the only one of the daycare kids who came back to thank my mother—at least two dozen of Miss Gladys's kids, now well into adulthood, still call her. That gesture always touches Mom, but she keeps things in perspective and points out a simple truth. "Imagine," she says, "if you're a child going into someone else's house and expecting them to take care of you. You'd be looking for nothing but a bunch of love." And more than anything, that's what my mother strived to provide.

Mom knew to adjust her caregiving style in dealing with different children, just as I've learned to fine-tune Elmo's tone depending on my audience. My parents naturally made the same kinds of adjustments in parenting me and my three siblings. While we were one very united family, we kids also happened to possess four extremely distinct personalities.

Take my brother, George Jr. The same fearlessness and drive that made him such a standout on the basketball court didn't translate as well off the court, mutating into a willfulness and devil-may-care attitude that got him into hot water more than once. One night in the 1970s, George set out for a party in a John Travolta–inspired ensemble. What afflicted him later wasn't *Saturday Night Fever* but plain old alcohol.

This story has grown legendary in my family due mostly to the role a neighborhood girl played in it. Mary Ann was over the moon pining for Georgie, but she was a bit of a tomboy with the muscles to prove it, a quality that came in handy. Fortunately for George, she was at the party and saw him pass out. Mary Ann simply hefted him over her shoulder and carried him across the rain-slick fields and streets of our neighborhood to get him back to our house, managing to keep George's beloved suit spotless.

I heard some commotion out on the steps and poked my head around the corner of the bedroom door. Mary Ann burst into the living room propping up Georgie.

My father thanked her for delivering the goods in fine order. Then he steered my brother to the couch and waited for him to come out of his stupor.

"So, you like to drink?" Dad asked.

My father went into the kitchen for a six-pack of Pabst Blue Ribbon, which he set on the coffee table.

"Have another drink, son."

Georgie waved his hand in surrender. "Can I go to bed, Dad? I don't feel too good."

"Not till you've had a nightcap. I insist!"

George Jr. never had another episode like that one again. My dad had made his point—that drinking to excess was a nasty habit; that it wasn't romantic and it didn't make you into a grown-up. Dad knew that George was strong-willed and he could take this kind of approach with him, but it would never have worked with Ne-Ne.

Ne-Ne lived for praise. As overachieving in the classroom as George was in the gym, Ne-Ne was strong-willed and held a high opinion of herself and her abilities. We still talk about the time she told the teacher who gave her a C in a Black History unit that the grade couldn't have been right because she knew more about the subject than he did. She employed her sharp tongue on the rest of us and was a master of verbal manipulation. Many times Pam and I felt the wrath of Ne-Ne. (She once tossed all my puppets out the window and into the snow; I got back at her by pitching all her cosmetics out after them.) Funny thing was, though, she demonstrated the territoriality and maternal instincts of a big cat. If anyone else insulted or teased us, she verbally pounced on the offender, making her usual wrath look like a love note.

Pam and I shared an artistic bent and a sensitive nature. As the baby, Pam endured a lot of teasing. Ne-Ne seemed to take particular delight in telling her that she was a little wet chicken we'd seen along the side of road and felt sorry for and took in. Out of earshot of Ne-Ne, I'd tell Pam not to mind what her big sister said. Like me, Pam loved to make things. As soon as she learned how, she'd make elaborate clothes for her huge collection of Barbie dolls. Eventually Pam tapped in to her creativity and love of clothing and playing dress-up to go into fashion design.

Whether they were cheering Georgie on from the bleachers as he raced down a basketball court, or sitting in an auditorium for one of Ne-Ne's modern dance performances or award ceremonies, or keeping Pam and me fully stocked with art supplies, fabric, and odds and ends to feed our creativity, my parents always found a way to support and love each one of us. Society was still sending a loud message that black children like us didn't have much to aspire to, but that negative talk was drowned out by our parents, who taught us that our dreams were worthy simply because they were ours.

Mom and Dad also knew that with big dreams comes the potential for big hurts. When you love someone you want to protect that person, particularly if it's a child, but like all parents, they couldn't protect their children from every hurt and they knew it. I've seen the devastating effects of peer pressure, and now that I'm a parent myself, I'm able to see this issue from a different perspective. I've also come to admire how my parents performed a delicate balancing act of protecting but not isolating us.

In my neighborhood, boys my age did one of two things: They either played drums or did sports. Of course the kids used to make fun of me and my growing interest. "Look at him, he's playing with dolls. He sews. He sleeps with his puppets," they'd taunt. Even my mother's friends would chime in, saying "Gladys, get that boy out of the house. He needs to play with the other kids."

Somehow, though, the sting of those remarks didn't last very long. My house was always a safe haven, the one place where I felt accepted and where everyone understood my interest in building puppets. Because my parents treated me and my budding passion with respect—showing their support by driving me to hobby shops and fabric stores for supplies, taking me to my first gigs as a performer, and encouraging me to make contact with professionals who would ultimately help further my career—I must have developed a thicker hide than most kids my age. Over time, the teasing and taunting had little effect because I felt so protected and secure in my parents' love, and I genuinely didn't care what the other children (or their mothers and fathers) thought of my hobby.

When the kids realized they weren't getting to me in a way that would cause me to stop doing what I loved, eventually they just left me alone. "He's being creative and building things," my parents would tell the other parents. "If he's enjoying himself, we don't really care if he's out playing with other kids or not." My family taught me that it was right to ignore the clamor of the crowd and go your own way.

I received this message over and over: You are loved just as you are. As an adult, I have never forgotten the value of that, and it's a message that Elmo and I try to express as frequently as possible.

By the time I was fifteen, I was capable of staying up all night, sitting at our kitchen table working on puppets. My mother, a gifted seamstress who even made fabric coverings for her shoes to coordinate with her dress, taught me to sew on her old Singer; my father helped me build puppet stages out of scrap wood he'd salvaged. I found materials to build puppets with and spent whatever money I had on supplies. Surrounded by piles of felt, fabric scraps, fake fur, foam, and glue, I could sit for hours happily lost in building puppets.

Once I snatched my mother's fluffy beige bedroom slipper, bending it in the middle before transforming it into a hand puppet. When I showed her that I'd turned that slipper into a puppet named Rocky, making it sing and dance to Neil Sedaka's "Laughter in the Rain," she forgave my thievery with a smile. Little did she know that this was just the beginning of my making off with personal items in the name of puppet creation. I think of it now: What few material possessions my parents had, I was eyeballing—and going after with a pair of scissors! But they hardly batted an eye.

. . .

"WHEN YOU'RE A parent, everything changes. You'll see things differently—just you wait." Over and over, after my wife and I found out we were going to have a baby, we'd hear those words, and truth be told, we'd roll our eyes. But, of course, those folks turned out to be right once our daughter, Shannon, was born. We immediately began to look at the world differently, to consider the needs of someone other than ourselves, and to give those needs top priority. (We quickly learned that when a diaper needs to be changed, it needs to be changed *now*, not at the next commercial.) We worried about different things, after Shannon. We found joy in different things, after Shannon. And most of all, we had an increased capacity to give and receive love, after Shannon. Though Genia and I are now divorced, our child brought love into our lives in a way we never expected.

At this point—ten years into Elmo's life and five years before "Elmo's World" would debut—the fuzzy red monster was already a big part of my life, as were children. By now, I'd worked for and with kids for most of my life, but I never really thought about being a parent myself.

When I found out that Genia was pregnant, I was overjoyed to know that I was going to be a father. I wanted to see my baby right then and there! I had no idea nine months could take so long to pass. Elmo was an important part of my life, and I was eager for this brand-new child to meet him. Genia had a fantastic job as an oncology nurse at a Johns Hopkins–affiliated hospital, which kept her in Baltimore; I was in the thick of it at *Sesame Street* in New York, five days a week. When I came home on the weekends, I could hardly wait to talk to our baby, though for now I thought it was fun for Elmo to do some of the talking. Genia would be lying on the couch, and I'd sit next to her on the floor so Elmo could snuggle up to her growing belly and tell her all about her parents: how we met, where we lived, who her grandparents and aunts and uncles were.

"Baby," Elmo would say, "your daddy can't *wait* for us to get together!" In my mind, the meeting of Shannon and Elmo would be the union of two of the most powerful love forces in the universe.

In my heart, I knew Elmo was reaching my baby girl, but I wanted to do more to welcome her into the world: I wanted to do a video diary told from Elmo's point of view. When the big day arrived, and we knew it was time to head for the hospital, I called both our moms and Ne-Ne, and helped Genia get ready to go. Then I ran down to the workshop to get Elmo and the video camera. "This is it, baby!" he said to the camera. "You're going to arrive today!"

By now Genia's mom had arrived at our house, along with Ne-Ne (who had to do some of the Lamaze sessions in my absence, and who is still as close to Genia as any sister). Genia's contractions were progressing and it was time to go. As I videotaped everyone preparing to leave, I had Elmo say "And there's your grandmommy and your Auntie Ne-Ne getting into the car to take you to the hospital." I panned the camera over to Genia and had Elmo say "And there's your mommy!" In the background, you can hear Genia saying "Put the damned camera down and get in the car!"

I wanted all of those memories to be preserved in a special way. When Shannon was still a baby, I asked a talented director and editor named David Gumpel, who worked with Jim Henson, to do for me what he'd been doing for his own kids for a while. He put together a music video from the footage I shot over the course of Shannon's first year. He spliced in some of our still photographs with my video, for a very special presentation. But I wanted more. Lilias White, a Tony award-winning actress and friend, and a regular on *Sesame Street*, sang a song Jill Scott wrote and arranged called "Sha Sha My Baby."

I treasured that video and frequently shared it with a very young Shannon. I knew that she had no memory of those events, but it had been such a special, magical time for us and we wanted her to know how much she was loved. As a little girl, Shannon seemed confused by it; I really think she felt some connection, but she didn't know why. It scared her, and we couldn't show it to her. Over the years, that video has been relegated to a shelf, but every now and then when I get the urge, I watch it and relive the joys of those baby days.

I remember an exhausted but happy Genia and me, shortly after Shannon's birth, relaxing with the baby asleep in her bassinet. When you're a brand-new parent, you can happily pass a lot of time just looking at your baby. Shannon's face was creased with that classic newborn frown, but she looked so angelic with her downy halo of hair. I don't know if I have the words to explain what happened to me in that moment, but it was as if I were truly seeing her for the first time. Until then, it had been almost as if I had been seeing her through Elmo's eyes—I'd so often used Elmo's voice to talk to her in the womb, to narrate the video.

Suddenly I didn't feel the need to have Elmo speak for me. I could just be Daddy with our child in that moment. I don't know if, in those months leading up to Shannon's birth, I'd used Elmo as my messenger because I was afraid and unsure of what to expect as a father. I knew I could trust Elmo to reach her since he rarely failed to touch the heart of any child he met. He'd gotten me this far, but now it was time for Kevin to do his job as a father, and it was a task I took to with a passion.

That night, for the first time, I told my darling little girl that I loved her in my own voice, one on one, eye to eye, and soul to soul. She opened her eyes and smiled at me—I don't care if some people tell me it was just gas.

I thought I'd known love before, but I'd never felt anything like this. I'd seen how my mom shared her love with children, both her own and her daycare kids, and I'd tried to emulate her when I was performing Elmo. But in that intimate moment with Shannon when our eyes and hearts locked, I knew that with Elmo I was simply acting—yes, I was acting from the heart, basing my performance on my genuine love for children, on my happiest memories of childhood, and tapping a reservoir of good intent. But what Shannon and I shared then and ever since is no act, no trick of the camera.

Eight years later, flying home from MuppetFest, I thought about the sophisticated videotape I'd made of Shannon's first year, and of all the talented people I'd gotten to contribute to it. And then I thought again of that little girl who just wanted to see and touch Elmo and tell him how much she felt. How simple it is to express our love.

People ask me how being a father to Shannon has influenced my performance as Elmo. I tell them that each time I put Elmo on my arm, I am drawing on the completely unconditional and nearly mystical connection I feel with my daughter. It's true what those other parents told Genia and me all those years ago—being a parent changes everything.

Something inside me changed, as well, and for the better. Elmo had taken me to a marvelous place in my life, and after my daughter was born, it was time for me to take him even further.

THOUGH ELMO IS quick to say "Elmo loves you," he doesn't express his feelings through words alone. Elmo backs up his words with warm hugs and a gentle rain of kisses for any child who wants them.

Sometimes, for some kids, words simply aren't enough. Though I felt very loved and protected as a child, open displays of Elmo-style affection weren't a part of our family culture. This is not uncommon even in the closest families. It's just personal. When I first started working with Elmo and people brought their kids on set, or I was doing a live appearance, I was stunned by the transformative powers of a loving touch.

When I'm doing a live appearance with Elmo, the kids don't really see me; they are focused on their buddy. If I were to remain standing, they truly wouldn't see me because at six foot one, I tower over them. By necessity, to bring Elmo to the children, I have to get down on their level physically (and with my forty-five-year-old knees, it gets tougher every year). When I place Elmo in front of them, I'm amazed at what happens when I have him look directly into their eyes, put his arms around them for a hug or a kiss, or just caress a cheek or shoulder with one of his fuzzy red hands. As Elmo comes to life with these physical displays of affection, so do the children.

Though youngsters are far more uninhibited when it comes to accepting Elmo's love, he has a dramatic effect on many adults, as well. A few years ago, I was in Baltimore doing an appearance as a part of a Sesame Workshop educational outreach program. The room was filled with 154 educators and other professionals, parents, and concerned citizens who wanted to assist with our school readiness program. I was to be the unannounced guest speaker, and when I walked in with Elmo, that audience, who only moments ago had been engaged in a serious, issue-oriented discussion about education, suddenly transformed into a rowdy mass of preschoolers who wanted to hug and kiss the fuzzy red monster. I guess you're never too old to love.

Elmo's love has a magical way of traveling through TV sets, but when a child can physically touch him, the power of his love is magnified, as if it somehow becomes more real. Think of what happens when you touch another human being. When you reach out to hold someone's hand, or hug them or kiss them, you're affirming that your love truly exists.

I learned through puppetry that to make the illusion believable, the puppets have to interact physically with one another—and especially with humans in the performance. Whenever we have guest stars on *Sesame Street* who will be doing bits with Elmo, I remind them that in order for the performance to be authentic and credible, they have to touch Elmo and let Elmo touch them.

Elmo has taught me that on-screen or off, touch makes the magic of love more real.

THERE'S ONE LAST lesson on love I'd like to share, and that is that before you can love someone else, you have to love yourself. Through Elmo, I pass that message along. I learned it from my parents, who taught me the importance of self-respect early in life. With that belief in myself, I gained the freedom and courage to pursue the life I am trying to live now.

When I talk to children and young adults as Kevin—not Elmo—I always try to impress upon them the importance of having self-respect, of listening to their hearts and going after their dreams. I tell them a little about my background and how I got into puppetry, and then point out that my story mirrors the message of the characters on *Sesame Street*: No matter who you are—a big yellow bird, a grouch in a can, a frog in a trench coat, or a furry red monster—you can love and be loved and find your place in the world.

With Elmo as my partner, with my family as my inspiration, I've learned that love works best when we keep it simple, when we remember to say it and show it, and, most of all, when we share it.

2

JOY

NEARLY EVERY SUNDAY, we'd exchange worn jeans and T-shirts for carefully pressed clothes and shiny shoes, and pile into the family car—the 1919 Get Out and Push, as we kids called it—to gather as a family at the New Psalmist Baptist Church. When the reading was over, we'd get up on our feet for a pew-vibrating, hand-clapping, Lord-praising song. "Make a joyful noise to the Lord, all the lands . . ." I basked in the sound and fury of it all.

To me, there is no greater "joyful noise" than the sounds of music and laughter, and our home in Turner's Station was infused with both. Music was such a part of our lives that I can't recall our house ever being silent. It just made us feel good.

Dad and my Aunt Dorothy and Aunt Odessia sang in the church choir, and my uncles all sang in church, too. For me Sunday mornings meant services and a visit to my Grandma Banks's house in Baltimore. My Uncle Ed was confined to a wheelchair, so he couldn't attend church in person. I'd get to Grandma Banks's, and Uncle Ed and my grandfather would be watching services on their old Philco, their heads bobbing in time with the music.

I'd hang back in my shy style, but the gospel music was so moving my toe would start tapping and I'd start swaying, all caught up in the sounds of Mahalia Jackson singing "Move on Up a Little Higher."

I'd catch my grandfather's eye and drop my gaze, embarrassed. He'd come over to me, squat down, and put his arm around my shoulders. "Hey, Kevin, it's okay to show your love for something. If you feel it, let it show, especially if it's for the Lord."

Gradually, in the years to come, I'd learn there was no harm in letting my joy out. In fact, doing so would bring it back to me tenfold.

Gospel wasn't the only music I loved. Growing up as I did in the 1960s meant growing up with the sounds of Motown. I loved the Jackson Five, the Chi-Lites, The Stylistics, and Earth, Wind & Fire. I still can't help singing along in falsetto (Motown style, not Elmo style) when I hear "Oh Girl" and "Betcha By Golly Wow," and of course my feet get happy with "ABC."

As my musical tastes broadened, I got into jazz in a major way, listening to Dizzy Gillespie, Sarah Vaughan, and Billie Holiday. Louis Armstrong became a favorite, especially for his gravelly voice. One of the first *Sesame Street* characters I performed, before Elmo, was

Hoots the Owl (created out of a workshop with director Jon Stone). I based his voice on Armstrong's.

I wasn't alone in this joyful appreciation; everyone in my family loved music and whether we were gathered in front of the television set watching Ed Sullivan, listening to my dad's old 78 rpm Blue Note label albums or my sister Ne-Ne's latest 45, music was a nonstop presence in the Clash household.

While she was fixing dinner or sewing or just plain relaxing, Mom was never without a song. Even now, I can hear her singing, "Shoo Fly Pie and Apple Pan Dowdy makes your eyes light up, your tummy say 'howdy' . . ." Like all of us, she had a wide repertoire including tunes from the Carpenters to bluesy Dinah Washington and Mr. Nat "King" Cole.

If you came to my house on any given day, you'd hear music, and you'd also hear laughter. With so many kids underfoot—me and my siblings and our friends, mixing with my mother's daycare kids— laughter was inevitable (as were tears). I loved spending time with all the babies and little kids, entertaining them with my first puppets and making them laugh. Once I stepped away from that laughter and went out into the world, I became shy and withdrawn. In fact, I was so uncomfortably shy on some days that if I was walking down the street and saw somebody I knew coming toward me, I'd dash across the road to the far sidewalk.

But my shyness disappeared as soon as I slipped on a homemade puppet and entertained the other kids. I was too young to make sense of my split personality—the shy guy versus the entertainer—but I did know that from an early age, I had a strong urge to make others laugh and to bring them joy. Using my puppets, I rarely failed to get the reaction I wanted from my first audiences, and my confidence began to grow.

Over and over again, I'd watch entertainers on television and study them. On *The Mike Douglas Show*, I saw Richard Pryor, Totie Fields, and many other comedians do their thing. My dad would buy comedy albums—Pryor, Moms Mabley, and Redd Foxx (we weren't allowed to listen to some parts), and of course Bill Cosby. I listened to Cosby's classic live recording, *Wonderfulness*, till I practically wore the grooves off that record. I would laugh until I cried, listening to him recount the story of "Chicken Heart," and a few other hilarious bits. (Imagine how thrilled I was when many years later Elmo and I got to work with Cosby on *Sesame Street*.) The sound of laughter and applause was "wonderfulness" in itself, and more and more, I began to crave anything close to that type of audience response when I did my own performances for the kids.

I wasn't the only Clash kid on the prowl for a laugh. With Ne-Ne as our ringleader, Pam and I would peel price stickers off the groceries Mom would bring home. Once Dad was settled in his favorite chair for a quick predinner nap, we'd make our move, silently surrounding his sleeping figure and putting the stickers on his face. We especially loved to put one on his lip and watch it flutter as he breathed. We'd scatter and then Dad would wake up, rub his face, and come to dinner with a few bits of sticker clinging to his skin, totally oblivious. We'd sit around the table staring down at our food, our shoulders quaking. Mom was our accomplice, her trademark nervous sniffling masking her efforts to not crack up too soon.

"What's so funny?" he'd ask, and we'd bust out laughing as he touched his face.

Now we live in the Comedy Central era, so our kid-stuff stunt may not seem like much in the way of entertainment, but we got a huge kick out of seeing our dad with a .99 tag on his forehead, and the thought of it still makes me grin.

My dad liked to play a prank or two himself. One day he came home from work and, instead of going for his chair, he stood in the kitchen while we helped our mom get dinner ready, his long coat still buttoned up. I saw something bulging near his chest. I also noticed that he was standing funny, with his shoulders hunched up around his neck and his arms folded across his chest like he was freezing.

"Kevin, how was school today?" he asked, and this time the space just under his left armpit seemed to inflate.

I looked at him and saw that his eyes were dancing and the corners of his mouth were twitching. Something was up.

He kept asking Pam and me more how-was-your-day questions, and his coat was acting like Jiffy Pop on the stove. Suddenly I saw something brown poking out from the space between the buttons— a puppy's leg. My dad couldn't keep the little creature under control much longer, and he unbuttoned his coat and pulled out a tiny Chihuahua that we eventually named Pepper.

In the years to come, that crazy little dog would make us laugh as much as any comedian, but in that moment, it was my father who delivered the joy.

ELMO'S LAUGH, AS infectious as it is frequent, is an important part of his personality, and it's part of mine as well. When I feel happy, I often punctuate the ends of my sentences with laughter, just like Elmo, and I can think of no better expression of our joy than the uniquely human act of laughter. But unlike me, and like most three-and-a-half-year-olds, Elmo has almost no inhibitions about laughing. He never worries about what others may think.

Have you ever noticed how a lot of adults and even some kids, as they get older, look around when they're laughing and cover their mouths as if there's something wrong with it? Does being around somebody who has a great guffaw or a silly snort of a laugh make you uncomfortable, or do you want to join in?

You will never see Elmo hold himself back from laughing when he feels joy, though he is always careful never to laugh *at* someone. Elmo knows that sometimes laughter can be the cause of hurt feelings.

Elmo's laughter is an expression of pure pleasure and enjoyment. No matter how my day is going, when Elmo starts to laugh, I feel it, too. When I'm performing, I wear a headband with a microphone attached to it and I sit on a low-slung, wheeled platform, with Elmo on one arm that I extend over my head. It's a physically demanding position that must be maintained for long periods of time. I'm also watching along on a monitor; we use monitors to make sure that we are keeping the Muppets in the frame and that they are looking where they should be—at other characters, directly at the camera, or wherever their attention should be focused.

Despite the physical and mental concentration it takes to perform Elmo, his humor and sense of fun always get the better of me. Colleagues and friends who know what my real voice sounds like have told me that after Elmo does a bit and laughs, they can hear my laugh mixed in, reacting to what I've just seen on the monitor. His joy is that contagious.

His trademark laugh nearly didn't survive the evolution of his character. Before Elmo and I "met" on that day in 1985, he wasn't known for his laugh—he was known as a bit player on *Sesame Street*, a little monster who appeared infrequently and said "Yes, yes, yes!" in a boisterous child's voice, over and over again. No one is exactly sure of when or precisely how Elmo arrived on the set, but Jim Hensen wanted his world to be filled with creatures of all types and colors and, oddly enough, there wasn't a red monster. And we couldn't very well reflect the diversity of the Muppet world without a red monster, given that we had green, yellow, purple, and even blue monsters with googly eyes.

Elmo—who got that name early on, though he was more commonly referred to on the set as "baby monster"—was first performed by different puppeteers, including Brian Meehl, whose regular characters included Telly and Barkley. After Brian left *Sesame Street*, the little red monster was stored away in the Muppet Workshop (where the puppets were built). David Korr, a writer who was noodling around and looking for inspiration, came across him and was smitten. David began writing Elmo into various scenes, with Richard Hunt performing. It was Richard who had Elmo saying "Yes, yes, yes!"—until he became so busy with other duties that he said "No, no, no" to Elmo and tossed him my way.

My introduction to Elmo occurred at the tail end of taping for the 1985 season, and I'd performed him, complete with his new laugh, only a few times before we went on hiatus for the summer. I had a few months to think about who this new character would become and what his personality would be like. There were many directions I could go in, but I knew, above all, that I wanted Elmo to be bursting with enthusiasm and pure joy.

The creators of *Sesame Street* were interested in developing a character that younger viewers could identify with. While the show was aimed at older preschoolers, kindergartners, and children in the early primary grades, our research was showing that since its inception in 1969, *Sesame Street* had undergone a change in viewership so that we were attracting more preschoolers and toddlers. The audience was trending younger, and the production staff felt it would be appropriate to have a character—like Elmo—who would represent the smallest viewers. As a result, Elmo was cast as a three-and-a-half-year-old . . . a three-and-a-half-year-old who would laugh a lot.

Shortly after I'd taken over as Elmo, a well-intentioned producer took me out to lunch. She wanted to congratulate me on the success of Elmo and his increasing popularity. She gave me some very valuable advice, and I was able to put much of it to good use. Then the conversation turned to Elmo's laugh. She was concerned that maybe it was "too much." As a performer, you're constantly refining and reworking your performance, and feedback—positive or negative—is all a part of the process.

We talked about it a bit more, and I made it clear I was aware that Elmo's laugh teetered precariously on the brink of over-the-top. I also thought that was part of his charm. Just like a three-year-old who darts and retreats from the line of acceptable behavior that's been drawn for him, Elmo's laughter functions as his (and my) limit tester.

Elmo's laugh remained intact, and when five million Tickle Me Elmo dolls blasted off the shelves in 1996, his joyful noise made him a household name and eventually would lead to the creation of "Elmo's World," the fifteen-minute show within the *Sesame Street* show, that stars Elmo. I recorded the laugh for the Elmo toy months before it hit the shelves and had all but forgotten about its debut as I was juggling my roles as a full-time performer and dad, shuttling between New York and Baltimore, where Shannon was an energetic baby-monster-in-training.

One fall day, we went on a diaper-run to a Baby Depot store, where giant stacks of baby wipes and formula competed with strollers, cribs, and toys for floor space. With the kiddie Muzak blaring and all the children chattering, I almost didn't notice the enormous Elmo display, until Shannon spotted the doll. I squeezed Elmo's belly, heard his laugh, and then laughed along with him and Shannon. (And I put him in the shopping cart and took him home for her.)

In the same way that I can't imagine Elmo being any other color than his ebullient cherry red, I also can't imagine Elmo without his distinctive, joyful laugh.

IT'S A SATURDAY morning, I'm twelve years old, and I'm sitting in my usual spot in front of the television set watching *H.R. Pufnstuf.* My attention is divided between the TV screen and the kitchen, where my mom is folding laundry.

Groaning, I look at the clock. I want to get out of there. I *need* to get out of there. There's someplace I need to be, and I can't get there soon enough.

"Mom? Can I help you with that folding?"

"No, Kevin, you watch your show. We'll get there soon enough."

Finally she and my dad are ready to go, and I hop into the backseat of the car, my heart racing like a madman's. I fidget and my legs won't stay still until my mother, now seated in the front seat, turns around to face me. "Kevin, baby, be still. We'll get you there, okay?"

Glancing in the rearview mirror as he backs out of the driveway and then stops abruptly to tease me, my father gives me a little grin. He drives at his usual snail's pace as we set out for the Merritt shopping center, home of Jo-Ann Fabrics, where aisles and aisles of fabrics are waiting—including the perfect fake fur I need to make the bear puppet I have in mind.

The car's wheels barely stop in the parking lot before I'm out the door, headed for the store's entrance. Dad heads for a hardware store next door, and Mom tells me to wait up.

I pull the door open for her and make a beeline for the back, running the tips of my fingers across bolts of sturdy canvas, flannel, and khaki, before reaching the rolls of brocade, monk's cloth, poodle cloth, velvet, and other exotic species beyond my reach, literally and because of their price per yard. Mom knows what I'm looking for, and she knows these enormous rolls of expensive drapery and upholstery fabrics may be suitable for the lifesize "walk-around" puppets I hope to one day make, but for today they're out of the question no matter how much I lust for them.

I find reasonably priced fake fur in luxuriant shades of brown and black—exactly what I wanted—and when I get Mom's nod of approval, I go to the cutting table. I relish the satisfying *whump* the bolt makes on the table. Even today, I can still hear the sound of the clerk's pinking shears separating my treasure from the rest.

I recognize the woman across the cutting station from us waiting her turn. It's a teacher at my school, and instantly I'm embarrassed until she speaks to me in a kind tone. "I sure enjoyed your assembly presentation, Kevin. So did my class. What are you making now?"

Just weeks before, I'd brought some of my puppets to class and performed for a group of students. Despite my shyness, I was increasingly getting the urge to seek out a larger stage than our living room and a more attentive audience than the daycare children and the neighborhood kids.

My glee overcomes my embarrassment and I reply, "A bear."

"Can't wait to see it. Will you be bringing him to school for any other project?"

Knowing that her class enjoyed my show pleased me in ways that nothing else had. Even without an appreciative audience, I still would have made puppets. I still would have bounced up and down with joy when I found the right materials, running from the kitchen table to show my mother and father my newest creation. I took great pleasure in my work, but the teacher was confirming what I'd hoped: that others—unbiased strangers, not friends or family members—enjoyed it, too. That knowledge brought me immense joy.

The ride home took forever, now that I had everything I needed to make the puppet that had taken shape in my head. I felt the same rush when I'd go to hobby or craft shops, where I'd find other supplies I could use. Once I had the fabric, foam, and glue, I could barely wait to get from the cash register back to the kitchen table. Once in my "workshop," I'd spread out the raw materials and know that they were filled with possibilities limited only by my imagination and developing skills.

Giving that bear life and personality was a joy I would savor in the days to come. Now I was learning that when I unleashed my own joy—through my creations and performances—into the world, it touched others and then it came right back to me.

WHAT'S THE FUN of celebrating if you have to celebrate all by yourself? Joy, like love, is sweetest when it's shared with others. I learned this lesson when Elmo and I "went Hollywood" for the first time, in 1987.

I had been performing Elmo for a little over one full season and was increasingly comfortable with his growing role. I had his laugh and his voice down pat, and I was having a great time developing his character, tweaking here and there as we studied the reception he was getting from audiences. Genia and I were dating regularly, and were talking about building a life together. I was playing a principal and increasingly popular character on a major children's television show, and my future seemed set. I had many people (and puppets) to thank for helping me get to this point in my life and career, but none more than Jim Henson.

Jim Henson brought our profession out of the children's birthday party circuit and into the international limelight, and he revolutionized the scope and mission of children's television programming. As a puppeteer, entertainer, and artist, Jim ranked right up there with Edgar Bergen and Burr Tillstrom (the creative talent behind *Kukla, Fran and Ollie*). Given the phenomenal success of *Sesame Street*, *The Muppet Show* (which ran from 1976 to 1981), and *Fraggle Rock* (1983 to 1987), it's no wonder that in 1987 the Academy of Television Arts & Sciences (which awards the Emmys) inducted Jim into the academy's Hall of Fame as a member of its fourth class of honorees. To give you some idea of how great an honor that was, Jim's fellow inductees that year included the legendary Bob Hope, Johnny Carson, acclaimed oceanographer Jacques Cousteau, the hilarious television pioneer Ernie Kovacs, newsman Eric Sevareid, and ABC television network founder Leonard Goldenson. If a man is judged by the company he keeps, then Jim Henson was a living legend.

For a living legend, Jim was one of the most accessible and silliest men I've ever met. Those of us who knew him and worked with him are often asked what he was like. Universally, we respond that Jim was Kermit the Frog. He was as decent and funny an everyman (everyfrog?) as his beloved creation. Jim's main goal in life was to have fun. He brought that sensibility to the studio with him every day. Remember how Kermit was the center of the maelstrom of outrageous personalities and calamitous chaos on *The Muppet Show*? That's what working with Jim on any production was like. He gave us all such free rein to have fun, but whenever the clock told us it was time for the show to go on, we would get our act together. Even though we were enjoying ourselves, we knew how much it mattered to Jim that we entertain and inform our audience.

When I found myself on an L.A.-bound jet out of JFK International sitting among a group that included Frank Oz (Miss Piggy, Bert, Cookie Monster, Fozzie Bear . . .), Jerry Nelson (The Count, Sherlock Hemlock, Sgt. Floyd Pepper . . .), and a host of other Muppeteers, I was flying higher than Elmo's "cousins" from *Pigs in Space*. I'd never been to Hollywood before, never been asked to perform at an awards show, never been picked up at my apartment in a limo, and never had a room booked in my name at the Beverly Wilshire Hotel! Best of all, I was there to honor a man I loved and respected, and with me were some the finest puppeteers around—members of the cast from *Sesame Street, The Muppet Show*, and *Fraggle Rock*. We were all there as part of a musical number that would serve as a comic tribute to Jim.

We hung out in the lobby of the hotel, talking shop and laughing when we saw Richard Hunt, with his unruly, Muppet-like hair, getting into the limo with a pink napkin loaded with Danish he'd saved from his room service breakfast.

Later at the theater, though I tried to act nonchalant and professional, I was so fresh out of the box that I was in awe of all the film and TV legends who were present, from Harry Belafonte to Lucille Ball, and more than once I had to stop myself from staring.

I'd never worn a tux before—I'd made a miniature one for a puppet, but I'd never put one on myself—and there was a big difference. I could not figure out how to keep my shirt tucked properly into my cummerbund. The cummerbund either pooched out, giving me a potbelly, or pushed the shirt upward, providing me with a barrel chest. Who should come to my rescue but Jay Leno, who was backstage at the same time. "There's a button on the inside front of the pants that goes with a hole on the shirttail," he explained, "but that's too sophisticated. Just unzip your fly and pull your shirt down through there." I thought it was pretty cool of him to help—and not turn me into the punch line of a joke!

When it was time for our number, all the Muppets sang and danced in a full-blown production entitled "Jim." Though the tune has long since gone out of my memory, I can still remember the chorus of "da-da-da-da-da-da—JIM!" that we sang with lung-busting gusto. We wanted to raise the roof and bring the house down in tribute to our boss, mentor, and friend. When Harry Belafonte walked to the podium to deliver his introductory and laudatory remarks presenting Jim, I had a lump in my throat the size of Elmo. To imagine that I was a very small part of a pioneering organization nearly overwhelmed me. That someone I respected, admired, and called a friend was being honored brought me more joy than anything I'd experienced to that point. (Shannon was still years away.)

Though I wanted to stay, I had to be back in New York to do *Sesame Street*, so I shrugged out of my tuxedo shortly after our number was over to prepare for the red-eye home. Jim had gone to sit in a place of honor in the theater, so I didn't get a chance to tell him how happy I was for him, but I was confident that he knew.

THREE YEARS LATER I was busy shooting *The Muppets at Walt Disney World* on location when I heard I'd been nominated for an Emmy, for "outstanding performer in a children's series." I was stunned. Me? An *Emmy*? I had no idea I was even being considered for a nomination. Up until that point in my career, I rarely thought about things like winning awards. That was for other people, especially the ones who'd been at it longer than me.

I didn't even understand how the process worked until one of the show's producers explained it to me. The production staff got together and submitted a group of names to the Emmy committee, and the committee had chosen me as one of the finalists for my performance as Elmo. For the next step, I needed to select and submit a tape of an Elmo performance to the committee.

A favorite segment immediately sprang to mind. Alison Bartlett O'Reilly, who plays Gina on the show, is babysitting Elmo. She does all the usual things you do when you babysit a three-and-a-half-year-old. When she bathes him, Elmo imagines being Elmo Cousteau plumbing the depths of the tub, and he meets a policeman fish beneath the "sea" who helps him find the way back to the surface with the treasure—a bar of soap—he finds. Gina does a marvelous job of treating Elmo the way she would her own child. The tender, sweet moment when she tucks Elmo in, patiently overcoming Elmo's antics to stretch out his bedtime, ends the scene on just the right note of humor and tenderness.

The tape was sent off, and until I received formal notification of my nomination via a very impressive-looking mailed certificate, I didn't think much about the award at all. I was happy with the certificate itself and immediately had it framed and hung it in my workshop at home in Baltimore, fully expecting that was as far as it would go. The Daytime Emmys weren't as big a deal as they are now. And the children's television categories ranked low in the pecking order, beneath the soap opera and talk show awards. But I was still thrilled to be in the company of children's television greats like Fred Rogers, LeVar Burton (of *Reading Rainbow*), and Paul "Pee-wee Herman" Reubens.

From the time I was notified of my nomination in April 1990 to the announcement of the winners in September, we'd all suffered a great loss. Jim Henson died unexpectedly of a streptococcal infection on May 16 of that year. While we all carried on in the best tradition of Jim and remembered his mission to have fun, there were moments when we missed him terribly.

I was busy with work, Jim was gone, and given my competition, I didn't think I would win. I even forgot the exact date that it was to be held on, but I did ask director Ted May to accept the award for me if I won. "Just say 'Thank you, Jim,' " I told him.

I was in bed in Baltimore when the phone rang at 12:15 A.M. I picked it up and through the fog of half-sleep heard the voice of executive producer Dulcy Singer.

"Congratulations, kiddo. You won!"

It took me a minute to figure out what she was talking about, and suddenly I was fully awake, pleased and truly humbled. I couldn't go back to sleep because I was so excited. I called and woke up everyone in my family, all my friends, even my old high school drama teacher, Mr. Riggs. Back in New York, everyone at *Sesame Street* was gracious with their congratulations (Richard Hunt jokingly said that I owed him half an Emmy for tossing Elmo my way), and I felt proud to have the approval and appreciation of my peers.

When the statuette arrived at my house in Baltimore, I tore open the box like a kid at Christmas (except when I was a kid I would have carefully opened the box knowing I could have built something out of it later) and set it on a shelf. It was bright. It was shiny. It weighed a lot more than I thought it would. As I looked at it and considered what it represented—not just my work, but the work of the whole *Sesame Street* family—I felt like I had done Jim proud.

Jim had won countless Emmy awards over the years, and so had the show. Now I had one, too. When I stopped thinking of it as an individual award and started thinking of it as an award that I'd won as part of Jim's team, I felt even happier. I couldn't help thinking back to that night in Hollywood honoring Jim, almost three years to the day. So much had changed, but the joy of being a part of that group was intact.

Eventually, and especially after the creation of "Elmo's World" in 1996, I turned into the Susan Lucci of the children's television world—always nominated and never a winner after that first time. Since 1990, I had collected Emmys in the producing category, but I'd only won once for my work as a performer.

In May of 2005, I was in Negril, Jamaica, performing with Roscoe Orman (Gordon) at a beach resort on the night of the Daytime Emmy awards. Since I couldn't be at the ceremony, I arranged for Shannon, my sister Anita, and my friend Danette De Sena (who also did casting for *Sesame Street*) to attend in my absence.

"It's great just to get the nomination," I told Shannon, bracing her for the probability that I would lose. "If I don't win, it's okay. You'll all be there, celebrating the nomination together."

Roscoe and I had just finished the show and were headed back to our rooms to rest when we bumped into our sound engineer.

"Congratulations, Kevin."

I thought he was congratulating me for our performance, so I said, "Thanks. It was a good show. Thanks for your help."

"I don't work on your show."

He must have read the question in my expression. "The Emmy. You won. I'm congratulating you on the Emmy."

I was so busy with the show that I'd forgotten about the awards ceremony.

He pumped my hand, and Roscoe and I hugged. I started thinking about Shannon and Ne-Ne and Danette, wondering what the experience had been like for them, wishing I could have been there to share the moment. When I called my parents to tell them the news, Mom beat me to the punch. She'd seen the broadcast on television and was thrilled for me. She and Dad were also ecstatic about the fact that Shannon had been there. They'd seen her jumping up with Ne-Ne, Danette, and some of the *Sesame Street* gang, and my friend Emeril Lagasse had given Shannon a congratulatory hug.

"I can't wait for Shannon to tell me all about it in person," Mom said, reading my mind. I was so happy that I made more calls to family, friends, and colleagues. I talked for as long as I could, before I realized that Roscoe and I had dinner plans. I'm so grateful he was there to celebrate with me.

Later I remembered a conversation I'd had only a few months before with Frank Oz, during a shared cab ride. Like Jim, Frank was one of my idols, and one of the funniest men I've ever known, an accomplished professional with a stellar career. We had been talking about our work, about what a good life we both had, how fortunate we were to be doing something we enjoyed so much.

"You know what the best part is, Kevin? Yeah, I've done all these things I love, I couldn't be happier with this as a career. But what means the most to me is what I've been able to do for my family as a result."

I had only nodded in agreement then, but now I was saying to myself, "Amen to that."

When I got back home, no one came over to my apartment to hang klieg lights, no one was wearing a ball gown or a tux, and no television cameras were there to capture the moment. But I was bursting with pride when Shannon told me about her night at the Emmys and how excited she'd been when she heard my name called.

Eventually, the award itself arrived and I pulled it out of the box. As I held it in my hands, I thought about my parents, about the laughter and music that had been the soundtrack of my childhood. This one, I felt, was as much theirs as it was mine. The joy they'd given me had come full circle.

3

CREATIVITY

MY FATHER HELD the nub of a flat carpenter's pencil in his hand, the copy of *TV Guide* open to an ad for a correspondence art school, as he tried his hand at drawing "Winky." The ad featured a basic line drawing, but Dad went well beyond that and embellished the character with shading to give his drawing depth.

I was fascinated, watching his natural talents at work as he unknowingly gave me a lesson on the finer points of perspective and shadow. After a while, Dad would wad up the paper and push himself away from the kitchen table, yawning. In my young mind my father had produced a masterpiece.

Dad was content with doodling on a lazy Sunday afternoon, but I looked for opportunities to create on a daily basis, and often my best efforts unfolded in front of the TV. Drawing "Winky" was dandy, but

I wanted to get down on paper what I saw on the small screen. By the time I was six, I was spending hours in front of the television with my supplies gathered around me—sheets of paper, crayons, Magic Markers, and, occasionally, one of my Dad's treasured Marks-A-Lots, with its overpowering smell and brilliant color.

I'd watch *Kukla, Fran and Ollie*, Shari Lewis's Lamb Chop, the marvelous creatures on Sid and Marty Krofft's *H.R. Pufnstuf* or *The Banana Splits*, and, of course, later, all those curious Muppets from *Sesame Street*. I'd sit up-close as possible to the set (Mom was wrong—I'm proof you won't go blind) and study those figures as I drew them, trying to understand how on earth they made those puppets.

And I didn't restrict my viewing to children's television. I would watch *Petticoat Junction*, *The Brady Bunch*, *The Beverly Hillbillies*, or similar fare while wearing one of my puppets on my hand. I'd watch the screen and, at the same time, watch my puppet in the mirror that hung by our TV.

My goal was to perfect the facial expressions and mannerisms as well as move the mouth in sync with the voice on the screen. So, if Mr. Douglas on *Green Acres* was having a chat with Mr. Ziffel about keeping his pig Arnold out of the corn crib, I'd have put my puppet in one role or another, acting out the scene. There was no danger of me ever becoming a couch potato, because I seldom just sat there passively watching TV.

As another part of my "training," I was becoming a serious people-watcher, all in the name of trying to make my puppet creations as lifelike as possible. I probably stared at a lot of folks, but I wasn't being rude; I was just doing my homework, watching how people of all ages moved, spoke, emoted, and generally behaved.

As it turned out, the first key to my performance as Elmo was, of course, emulating the children I saw at home. And one of the things that I've always loved about children is their vivid, unrestrained, and far-reaching imaginations—the depth and breadth of their creativity.

"ELMO'S PACKED HIS suitcase and Elmo is taking a trip!" Elmo told viewers in his first appearance on the 1986 season of *Sesame Street*, when I began performing him as a regular featured character. By now I'd had a good chunk of time to think about his developing personality, as had the talented writers behind the show, and we were clearly on the same wavelength. Elmo, like the children who inspired his creation, was going to be a character who would make liberal use of his imagination!

In that very first scene, Elmo, dragging an imaginary suitcase, walked up to the workbench in front of the Fix-It-Shop, where Luis, played by Emilio Delgado, was repairing a toaster (the same toaster that never, ever seemed to get fixed, no matter how many scenes it was in). "Hi, Luis! I'm going on a trip! Can you help me with this suitcase?"

Elmo wasn't stopping at using his imagination to dream up his "trip." Like most freethinking children, he'd taken his creative play a step further and had packed his imaginary suitcase. He had crammed it so full that he couldn't close it, and now he'd come to the shop to have Luis help him fix the situation. Luis asked Elmo what he had in there, so that he could help Elmo decide what to keep and what to leave behind to get the suitcase closed.

Elmo began pulling out imaginary pairs of socks and holding them up for Luis and the audience. Then he pulled out a few shirts, pairs of underwear, pajamas, and a whole host of necessities for his travels. Luis kept looking to the camera with one eyebrow lifted and a smile creasing his face, just going along with Elmo's flights of fancy. Little did any of us know just how overstuffed Elmo's imagination would turn out to be.

Each time I dipped Elmo's head so he could reach deeper into that imaginary suitcase, it was as if I were reaching deeper inside my own experiences as a child, thinking of the games we invented and the fun we had playing creatively. I also thought of other children, especially a memorable little boy named Ryan who was a regular at Mom's daycare. Ryan was a super-animated bundle. I decided that Elmo was going to be a lot like him.

As the cameras rolled, I was prepared to be the highest-energy three-and-a-half-year-old ever. I let myself go and felt an instant connection to Elmo. No longer was I channeling a version of Ryan or any other child. I was fully in the moment, inhabiting the mind and expressing the emotions of a little red monster who was determined to be fully prepared for his imaginary trip.

Though we stuck to the script and got the show's curriculum goals accomplished, before I knew it I was pulling a few things out of my own imagination and Elmo was tugging them out of his suitcase. After Snooks the floor manager yelled, "Cut," I saw our cameraman Frank Biondo laughing, and I knew I was on to something. Elmo and I were clicking. I could never have predicted how big the Elmo phenomenon would grow to be, but every journey, real or imagined, starts with a few tentative steps, and like most children, I took those first steps at home.

DRAWING, LIKE PUPPET-MAKING, was a childhood passion that gave me a sense of control, a feeling that I was able to master my environment, which is a crucial component of growing up. Think about toddlers' first successes at walking on their own or feeding themselves, the insistent "Me do it" that peppers most of their sentences as they attempt to do things without a grown-up's help, and I'm sure you'll see what I mean.

For me, being able to put down on paper something that previously existed only in my imagination was a pleasure, but it also gave me confidence—the confidence I needed to take even greater creative risks and strides. Even now, each success I have as a performer and artist feeds my desire to try new things and push the boundaries of my creativity.

In school, art earned me the positive attention that I craved as a child. Teachers recognized my creative ability, and I was constantly asked to illustrate the bulletin boards that decorated the classroom. Whether the theme was the first day of spring or something we were studying, I was selected to bring those images to life. I wasn't always the best student, but my teachers appreciated my skills (as well as the fact that I didn't doodle during lessons).

I drew, I imagined, and then I built the puppets that were beginning to fill every square inch of my space in our shared bedroom and overflowing onto yellow shelves in my parents' bedroom. The Clash kids were being crowded out by heaps of fur, jars of buttons for eyes, chunks of foam, and puppets with names like Skylow, Bartee, Moandy, Rocky, and Artie. (Sometimes I named my puppets for friends or people I knew—Bartee was named for a crazy-funny kid named Tony Bartee, and Skylow for a super-cool classmate with the tallest Afro.)

By the time I was a teenager, I was known around the community as the kid with the puppets. Often I was asked to perform at school, for fundraising events, at fairs, cultural festivals, and other venues, and even on a locally produced children's television show, where my old shy self would vanish once I had a puppet on my arm and an audience to win over. Though I didn't think about it this way at the time, I was getting a taste of success as a performer, and I wanted more.

When I was seventeen, a wildly creative artist who gave me a major push into the world I live in today came into my life, via my favorite medium—the television—and with the help of one of my creative fairy godmothers, my mom. I was watching (at this point, it was more like studying) a children's show called *Call It Macaroni*, scoping out the characters and entertainers. One of their regular segments featured a young boy or girl spending a day with a person in a featured profession. And that day, the featured professional happened to be the charmingly named Kermit Love, an accomplished costume designer and artist who worked with choreographers like George Balanchine and helped design and build Big Bird and Snuffleupagus.

I knew kids could get away with making stuff, with indulging their imaginations, but this guy was no kid. I was thunderstruck as I watched him give a tour of his workshop. Kermit Love had a Jo-Ann Fabrics store in his own workshop! He had racks of fake fur and sheets of foam in one area, and in another a stable of sewing machines. After the show was over, I sat in stunned silence as the credits rolled, and then the adrenaline kicked in. I went out in the yard where my mom was playing with some of the daycare kids.

"You won't believe what I just saw, Ma," I started. "This man was *amazing*. Who knew there was a place like his workshop? I mean, I guess they have to build Big Bird *somewhere*, but it blew me away—I have to see it for myself, Mom, I just have to. This guy had *everything*—materials, machines, shelves of supplies up to the ceiling . . . and the puppets, you wouldn't believe the puppets . . . and get this, this is his *job* . . . he makes a living doing this stuff." She listened patiently and with interest as my mouth ran a mile a minute, heading back into the house with the kids while I trailed behind, still spewing like someone who'd had a religious experience.

After she gave me the "calm down, Kevin" look she'd perfected, Mom called the local PBS station that broadcast *Call It Macaroni*. It helps to have a fairy godmother who knows how to use the yellow pages and cut through the switchboard operators and receptionists. After hours of creative wrangling, cajoling, and yarn-spinning about her talented son, she got Kermit Love's phone number in New York.

We left a message for Kermit, who called back soon after. He could not have been more gracious and encouraging. "So you saw the show! And you want to be a puppeteer? I know a thing or two about that." We spoke for about ten minutes as I answered his questions about my kitchen-table puppets and the local gigs I was doing. Before hanging up he invited me to come up to his workshop for a visit. As luck would have it, our senior class trip was to New York City, and my teachers agreed to allow me some time for a brief meeting with Kermit.

In person, his Greenwich Village workshop was even more astounding than it was on television. I couldn't believe that someone could have entire rooms devoted to things like fake fur and feathers. I dreamed of having such a space—I was making more and more puppets, including lifesize walk-around puppets that didn't exactly fit on a shelf. I could barely carve out a few square feet in our shared bedroom for a workspace, and the kitchen table was off limits by the time I got home from school, since we were either fixing or eating dinner or doing homework. I no longer was comfortable perched in front of the TV—I was close to six feet and still growing, and my long legs took up a lot more floor space these days.

To me, the word "network" meant CBS, not "potential job contact," but I was so wowed by our meeting that I knew enough to keep in touch with Kermit Love, who—on top of that name, his real one—bore an uncanny resemblance to Santa Claus. (He actually appeared in many photo shoots at the time as Jolly Old Saint Nicholas!) Kermit certainly gave me and countless other puppeteers the gift of his time, expertise, and guidance. Shortly after I visited his workshop, he did something wonderful for me that would completely alter the course of my life! He arranged for me to be invited to participate in the 1979 Macy's Thanksgiving Day Parade.

As the builder of Big Bird, Snuffy, and other Muppets, Kermit was closely connected to *Sesame Street* and Jim Henson. (Incidentally, Kermit Love had nothing to do with the name for Kermit the Frog, who was purely Henson's creation. Like his resemblance to Santa, Love's given name was just another appealing quirk that made him so special.) That year, Jim, Frank Oz, Jerry Nelson, Dave Goelz, Richard Hunt, and Steve Whitmire—the core Muppeteers—were performing on the *Muppet Movie* float to promote the launch of the film, and many of the *Sesame Street* characters were literally in need of warm bodies, or hands, actually. I would be a sort of Muppet temp on the *Sesame* float, filling in where needed. My parents didn't hesitate to let me work the parade.

My parents drove me to the train station the evening before Thanksgiving, and as I got out of the car, they wished me good luck. "We'll be watching you on TV, Kevin," Mom said. "Be safe, son," Dad added. "Enjoy this. And remember it for the rest of your days."

I **WAS SO** wired on the train up to New York that I couldn't relax or focus on anything. I was overwhelmed by one thought, and one thought only: Here I was, a kid from Baltimore, on my way to the big city to step inside a world that had previously existed only in my imagination. Better than that, I was about to spend the *night* in that world because Kermit had arranged for me to crash at his workshop on Great Jones Street! Cheaper than a hotel, and loads more fun.

I took a cab from Penn Station to the workshop. Kermit had a pull-out futon in the office area, and I dutifully got ready for bed, trying to avoid the temptation to poke around. Even though I'd been warned to get some rest in preparation for a long morning that would start early, I simply had too much adrenaline and too much on my mind. *I'm going to be in the Macy's parade tomorrow . . . me! In the Macy's parade.* I couldn't sleep and I abandoned the futon, giving in to my urge to check things out.

I'd seen his workshop before, but I hadn't seen the puppet-making area, and now I was standing in it. Though Big Bird and Snuffleupagus sprang from Jim Henson's imagination, Kermit Love and his builders actually constructed these larger-than-life creatures, and here were the ingredients that went into his creations. I had never seen so much foam in my life. What captured my imagination the most were the wings waiting to be feathered, and Snuffy, who was draped over the roof's rafters and gazing down at me like a giant guardian angel—albeit a funny-looking one.

I wandered around some more and drank it all in, then went to sit at one of the worktables at the front of his studio, and dreamed of the day I could design my own workshop. I was mentally taking notes of everything I'd seen, and was preparing my list of must-haves. I was in my element. I was home . . .

The phone rang and I jumped like a puppet myself. Without thinking whether it was for me or not, I answered it.

"Kevin? It's Kermit, just making sure you got in okay. You need to get some sleep now. We have a big day tomorrow." It was as if he'd known I'd been in a dreamy state, and now he was calling me back down to earth. I promised to hit the sack, and, somehow, I managed to fall asleep.

By six the next morning I was awake and riding in another cab, this time heading toward Seventy-ninth Street and Central Park West, where the parade would kick off. Nothing and no one could have prepared me for what I saw once I got close to the parade's starting point. Rows and rows of tour buses belched out bleary-eyed tuba players, drummers, baton twirlers, flag girls, and cheerleaders. For a few blocks, it seemed that every pedestrian was a member of a marching band.

I got dropped off a few blocks from where the *Sesame Street* float was stationed. I was a little early so I wandered the streets near Central Park until I saw the Museum of Natural History looming in front of me. In the predawn light and the orange and blue glow of the streetlamps, I saw several enormous shapes writhing on the ground. When I got closer, I could see these were the famous balloons, weighted to the ground. I stepped around a barricade and showed my official parade pass, my eyes agog as Kermit the Frog rose as if from slumber and stretched to his full length. I thought of all the sketches I'd done of him and wondered at the enormity of the scale of his construction. How did they put something like that together? I didn't have time to consider the methods for too long, though. I had a float to catch.

Traveling along Central Park West and then down Broadway performing Cookie Monster was an amazing experience. I practically got chills putting this professionally made and very famous puppet on my arm. Now I could look at the construction of a Muppet up close, not through a TV screen. The materials were of much higher quality than what I used back home. But puppeteering is puppeteering, and Cookie Monster worked pretty much the same way that puppets like Bartee did, so I poked Cookie's head out through the curtain of the float and went to work. Despite the fact that I spent the parade in an enclosed structure, I still had a good view through a small gap in the curtain; it was the largest crowd I'd ever seen, and certainly the biggest audience I'd ever had.

By all rights, I should have been exhausted. I'd barely slept, I'd gotten up when it was still dark, I'd ridden in a cramped float for five hours traveling at a very slow pace, and I had nearly lost my voice performing Cookie, too excited to realize no one could hear me over the noise of the parade. Then I'd gone to a reception for the parade participants (where I briefly met Jim Henson), but when it was all over, I was ready to do it again. I wanted to get up and do it every day of my life. On the train ride back to Baltimore, I relived every moment of my visit, knowing that I had much to be grateful for on that Thanksgiving. And though I would go on to perform in the parade many times, nothing ever matched that pulsating, life-changing first trip down Broadway to Herald Square.

ONE OF THE most imaginative endeavors I've ever been involved in is "Elmo's World," a colorful, lively celebration of creativity, presided over by one of the most inventive little monsters on *Sesame Street*.

Start with the set, for instance. Instead of an elaborately realistic backdrop like *Sesame Street*'s, with its brownstones, sidewalks, stores, and other lifelike interiors and exteriors, "Elmo's World" takes place in a crayon drawing of a universe as conceived by Elmo himself, though it was actually Mo Willems, one of the *Sesame Streets* writers, who dreamed it up. Through a mix of computer-generated graphics and live action, the line between "reality" and "pretend" is blurred. Elmo can move freely between these two worlds, until they are an inseparable combination of both. Simply watching "Elmo's World" encourages kids to incorporate elements of their imagination and their reality into a seamlessly rich and stimulating environment that they choose to create.

"Elmo's World" sprang from the fertile imaginations of some truly creative writers, including Judy Freudberg, Tony Geiss, and supervising producer Arlene Sherman. In 1998, *Sesame Street*'s thirtieth season, Elmo and I got our big break.

As I've mentioned, for the last three decades, *Sesame Street*'s audience had gotten steadily younger, and our research indicated that children struggled to pay attention to the show after about forty minutes. Three-year-olds had once been our youngest viewers, but now the show was attracting large numbers of two-year-olds and even babies as young as ten months. The magazine format of *Sesame Street* was confusing to these younger viewers, and as a result their attention was wavering.

The show hadn't had a major format change since its inception, and there was trepidation about tampering with the formula. But *Sesame Street* creator and visionary Joan Ganz Cooney has always advocated experimentation and innovation. *Sesame Street* was made more theme-based, and a more predictable format was created so that children could navigate the show more easily.

Elmo, whose popularity among toddlers and preschoolers had been borne out by the success of the Tickle Me Elmo toy two years earlier, was going to be the focus of the last fifteen minutes. The target audience would be two- to four-year-olds—in other words, Elmo's peers. The creators consciously geared it to this younger audience, while retaining the award-winning *Sesame Street* sensibility. And so, "Elmo's World" got its own set—that childlike crayon drawing brought to life through state-of-the-art animated special effects. Elmo would interact with two friends who would let him do all the talking: Dorothy, his goldfish, and Mr. Noodle, a silent film–era tramp inspired by the likes of Charlie Chaplin and Buster Keaton, brilliantly brought to life by the talented Bill Irwin.

When I learned that Elmo was being given his own show within *Sesame Street*, I was elated. Professionally it meant new challenges, including the opportunity for me to indulge my urge for creative risk-taking. There would be no adult narrating or explaining Elmo's point of view; rather, Elmo would lead the child through the show. Each episode would be like a playdate between the child and Elmo. I felt that the intimacy of "Elmo's World" would be a tremendous teaching tool. And I knew it would be a lot of fun to draw on my own imagination in bringing Elmo to life in this new way.

"Elmo's World" first aired on November 16, 1998, and was an instant success. Elmo's vivid color and high-pitched voice held children's attention, as did the fascinating set design and the show's thoughtful, interactive structure. This furry little guy truly represented a three-and-a-half-year-old—someone the youngest viewers could identify with. His interests—making friends, learning to dance or make music, brushing his teeth—were their interests, and he struggled with the same issues as they did, from sharing toys to going to the doctor or trying a new food.

Children (and their parents, teachers, and caregivers) fell in love with Elmo. It didn't take long for the cherry-red Muppet to skyrocket into the realm of my heroes, Kermit, Big Bird, Grover, Bert and Ernie, and Oscar the Grouch.

MY MOM AND dad were creative, but not just in the artistic sense. They frequently called on their imaginations in their day-to-day roles as parents, teaching and disciplining us in some nontraditional ways.

Dad took care of our lawn as best he could, but there was a shady, barren patch beneath a large weeping willow tree that was nothing but dirt. My father put it to use in his own unique style. Before I learned to read, my father would take me out into the backyard and stand me near that dusty patch of soil. He'd take a stick he'd whittled to a sharp point, and he'd scratch out the alphabet in the dirt. While he formed the letters, he'd say them out loud and have me repeat them. When he was done with the Z, he went right back to the beginning to the letter A and made up a twenty-six-word story using one word beginning with each letter. "Alex Bagby Can Dance Everywhere Feet Go Hopping . . ."

Imagine my surprise when, many years later, when I first heard Big Bird sing the alphabet as a word because he didn't understand what the letters represented! "ABC-DEF-GHI-JKL-MNOP-QRSTUV-WXYZ! It's the most remarkable word I've ever seen."

My dad was not a speech giver, even when it came to discipline, and as the father of four rambunctious kids, he did have to discipline us from time to time. If he wanted to make a point, he preferred doing rather than talking, which is how he came to teach us a lesson involving self-control and a very important, very cold bottle of ginger ale. We never went hungry, but sometimes we had to get creative with whatever was left in the refrigerator. Mom and Dad always sacrificed to make sure we were well fed and clothed, putting our needs ahead of their own. But even that had a limit, especially when it came to highly prized beverages.

Like most kids, we loved soda, but it disappeared as quickly as it showed up. One night, when I was about six, Dad took his personal bottle of ginger ale, which we were instructed never to touch, out of the refrigerator and marked the level of the liquid on the bottle with a dark line.

The next afternoon when he got home from work, he went into the kitchen and then came back out and made an announcement: "Everybody in the car." I got excited thinking we were going someplace fun. My mom asked him where we were going, but he simply shushed her and got us kids out the door.

"George! George!," Mom called to him from the front steps as my brother and sisters and I jumped into the car. "You're taking this too far!" she said with a nervous laugh.

But off we went with Dad, thinking he was taking us on a great adventure. Thirty minutes later, we were parked in front of the Baltimore City Hospital's emergency room.

"Okay, everyone out of the car. We're going to get your stomachs pumped so I can find out who drank my ginger ale."

Ne-Ne had her arms folded across her chest defiantly, Pam and I were looking at each other, completely clueless, and Georgie was squirming. Finally, close to tears, he confessed.

No one ever took a slug from my father's ginger ale again. Very creative parenting, don't you think? No yelling, no hitting, just an unforgettable reminder to mind his word.

It takes a creative mind to put a positive spin on a child's more, uh, hands-on endeavors. I probably spilled gallons of Elmer's glue on the living room carpet, and who knows how much ink, pencil, and crayon wound up on surfaces other than paper, but my mother took it all in stride, knowing full well that a tipped-over jar of paint or spilled glitter was an accident.

It's a good thing my father was equally tolerant of my creative urges, which sometimes simply overwhelmed me. When I was about twelve, I got possessed by "monkey fever." I didn't have any suitable material to make my monkey, but my mind flashed on the lining of my father's Sunday-go-to-church overcoat. It was made of a plush black synthetic fur piling—absolutely perfect monkey fur. Only after my scissors had done their handiwork and I'd cut that lining out of the coat and finished the puppet did I come out of my "must-create" fog. Lord, what had I done?

I knew I was in for it, and I didn't want to wait until Sunday when my father went to put his coat on, so I took the monkey and put it on the dresser in my parents' bedroom. Then I went into our room and sat on the bed awaiting my fate.

A little after five I heard my father come home, and I prepared myself for the worst. Five minutes later, I heard footsteps coming down the hall, and my heart boomed in my chest. My father loomed in the doorway, cradling the monkey like a baby in his arms.

My father wore his sternest look. He held out the monkey to me. "What's his name?"

I croaked out, "Moandy."

He took another step toward me and gently handed me Moandy the Monkey. His expression softened, he nodded and said, "Next time, ask," and turned and walked out of the room.

A moment later, I heard him ask my mother, "Did you see what Kevin made?"

"I saw he used up a good bit of your coat."

The two of them laughed but quickly shushed each other. Though they wanted me to learn a lesson and respect other people's possessions, I slept better that night because I knew they understood me.

Ruining a good coat was a creative risk I never dared attempt again. But I had glimpsed the depths of my parents' devotion to me and my dreams, and I can never thank them enough for all the truly creative ways in which they have contributed, and still do, to my success as an artist, entertainer, and person. They propelled me from one supportive environment to another—to *Sesame Street*, where creative risks are rewarded.

• • •

MY PERFORMANCE AS Elmo begins in the minds and imaginations of a team of highly accomplished writers. Even before the writers get started on a season's worth of shows, a lot of other talented people have their input in designing the curriculum messages for the season and for the individual shows. Dr. Rosemarie Truglio heads the Sesame Street Research and Education department, and she and her team are primarily responsible for the overall shape the season will take. Our producers, including Carol-Lynn Parente, Melissa Dino, Tim Carter, April Chadderdon, and others, are involved from the earliest stages of each show's creation and through every stage of production.

After the curriculum goals are set, head writer Lou Berger and his staff then structure stories with two main goals in mind: to educate and to entertain. Writers work singly and in pairs, and also in larger groups, and they share ideas and stories from their own experiences and the lives of children they know. A tremendous amount of back-and-forth and revision goes into even the shortest segments.

At this point, they sometimes ask the performers for input—many times they ask me if Elmo is capable of performing a certain action. I explain what he might or might not be able to do. Obviously, this is an incredibly collaborative endeavor. Everyone must set his ego aside in order to produce the best possible show. We're all involved in a fluid and fulfilling process with contributions from many minds, hearts, and experiences. Even when we have a final script, we're not done creating, and that's one of the great joys of working with Elmo on *Sesame Street*. During rehearsals, when we're out on the floor blocking scenes and going over dialogue, we can branch off in new and unexpected ways, delighting and surprising the cast, crew, creative and curricular team, producers, and ultimately our viewers. We regularly test content with those viewers—children are our best critics and teachers.

To some people, the technical side of a television production like *Sesame Street* may not seem as creative as elements such as the writing, acting, art direction, and puppeteering. But technology offers some amazing ways for us to expand the content. Advances in technology have meant increasing demands on the staff to keep up, but they've done so beautifully. I have an Elmo that I manipulate with my hand like a traditional puppet (I actually have nine Elmos, all of them capable of doing different actions). And now I also have an Elmo who is radio-controlled, not unlike a radio-controlled airplane.

It would be nice to think that there are no limits on our creativity at *Sesame Street*, but unfortunately, there is one: money. When we are trying to increase our use of technology behind the scenes, we sometimes hit a financial hurdle. After I'd done *The Adventures of Elmo in Grouchland* in 1999, which was Elmo's first movie, I really wanted to have a radio-controlled Elmo like the one we had made for the film. For the first time, I had been able to puppeteer Elmo without actually being underneath him, as I usually am.

I wanted to take that technology a step further, and I wanted an Elmo who could ride a tricycle on *Sesame Street*. In fact, I found and purchased what I thought was the perfect trike when I was in L.A. It wasn't just an ordinary red tricycle; it was a bright, multicolored design that fit the whole look of "Elmo's World." And another plus: It was adjustable with a frame and seat that could be expanded or made smaller, depending on the size of the rider. Of course, it had been designed for a growing child, but I thought it could be made just the right size for Elmo. Jason Weber, creative supervisor for the Jim Henson Company, and I made the request, but the production budget didn't allow for it. Finally, two years after I had put it on my wish list, complete with additional requests and follow-up reminders on file, we got the green light and funding to create our trike-riding Elmo.

I worked closely with Tom Newby, the genius electronic craftsman who designed and supervised the building of this new full-body Elmo, to make Elmo's movements seem natural and fluid. Finally, I got the call that our new friend was ready to go for a spin around the set on his three-wheeler.

Puppeteer Matt Vogel operated the tricycle via a small black box with an antenna and some switches. I used a radio-controller mitt to transmit signals to Elmo. Out he rode across the set, his legs pumping as he pedaled his colorful tricycle. I flashed back to when I'd taught Shannon to ride hers.

Matt had Elmo circle around the set and I had him turn his head, laughing gleefully, to look at all of us standing there like proud parents.

I love technology and am a gadget guy, and I pride myself on being pretty good at figuring out mechanical things, but I would never have been able to build an Elmo like this one! I wondered a bit about how that loss of the physical connection between us would influence my performance. I'm a hands-on performer, and this was revolutionary.

Advances like this in technology allow us to be more creative in our work. Executive producer Carol-Lynn Parente was so pleased with how this new Elmo had turned out that she had writer Molly Boylan and music director Mike Renzi create a song for him to sing as he rode his tricycle. When we finally filmed this scene, I directed and was especially pleased when Carol-Lynn and longtime director Ted May told me how much they'd liked it. We'd hit the right creative mix: classic music and lyrics, complemented by dazzling high-tech touches.

By embracing these new technologies, we're making Elmo real for millions of viewers. We wouldn't be able to do "Elmo's World" without blue- and green-screen technology, which allows us to enter characters into scenes and environments digitally (think of Elmo swimming in a fishbowl with Dorothy or flying through the sky as an Elmo pterodactyl that would otherwise be impossible, or too expensive, to produce without computers. These recent innovations are really no different from the standard lighting that illuminates our stage, or the sound and video editing machines that we use daily. Behind-the-scenes people like Dick Maitland, who does our sound effects, as well as the legions of staffers who operate the equipment, whether it's low tech or straight out of a computer lab, are no less creative than the performers and the writers. It takes the creative efforts of many to keep *Sesame Street* vital for a new generation of viewers.

My life growing up on New Pittsburgh Avenue wasn't so different from life on Sesame Street. Although I didn't have a dedicated professional educator like Rosemarie or a staff of writers, technicians, and directors, I did have my family, who helped me in all phases of the creation of my shows. I even had my own research team—the kids in my mother's daycare were always my first and toughest audience. I knew if I could make them laugh and hold their attention, then I was ready to take my show on the road.

Back then, each day began with the arrival of children—and that's the way it is on *Sesame Street*. And now, as then, I do my best to spark a fire and light their abundant imaginations.

MY PARENTS FED my creativity in a variety of ways, and I have tried to do the same thing with my daughter, Shannon, who happens to share my love of drawing. It's one of the things we did together when she was very young. One of my favorite activities was helping Shannon draw her day. We'd get out some paper and markers, and we'd go through her entire day, drawing scenes depicting each of the things she had done.

"So," I'd begin. "What's the first thing you did when you got up this morning?"

"I brushed my teeth, Daddy," she'd say, gripping her marker.

"Okay then, Sha. Let's see you draw that."

And off she'd go, making a picture of herself brushing her teeth, playing with a doll, eating her grilled cheese. In every picture, she'd always include her beloved dog, Buddy.

I loved the look of pleasure that washed across her face while she worked, the intense focus that softened into delight when she was done with each drawing. In looking at her, I saw myself as a child, the same feelings of satisfaction poured through me as I drew and created and built.

There's a certain sweet magic you feel when you sit down and create something with a child, whether it's a masterpiece in watercolors or pasta shapes glued to a paper plate. And remember, it doesn't matter if you haven't held a crayon in decades or if you don't remember how to fold a paper airplane or if you can't draw hands or horses or rocket ships. In the eyes of a child, your artistic talents are supreme. It's not *what* you create—it is simply the fact that you are helping that child celebrate the joy of creativity.

In a lot of ways, "Elmo's World" is very much like the imaginary worlds we all created as kids—whether we were in the driver's seats of our Hot Wheels cars, shopping with Barbie, or on the way to Pluto in our refrigerator-box spacecraft. Back then, we didn't hesitate to use our imaginations to go on imaginary trips, to pack up those imaginary suitcases and travel to faraway places that didn't exist on any map.

Elmo gives us grown-ups the permission kids never need to let our creative juices flow and maybe, just maybe, to reenter the world of make-believe and let some of our dreams come true.

4

TOLERANCE

WE HAD JUST left my grandmother's house in Baltimore City, where the violent riots of 1968, which exploded for several days in April following the assassination of Dr. Martin Luther King, Jr., were still sending aftershocks throughout the community. The major unrest—the fires, the looting, the street fighting—had come to an end, but the racial tension was still palpable, and even though I was just seven years old, I could sense the anxiety and the changes in the air. And I had seen the pictures in the paper and on the evening news—the screaming crowds, the cops in full riot gear, the armed soldiers standing atop the roof of the Sears building.

Dad drove the car slowly down my grandmother's street, warily eyeing the groups of whites and blacks who stood on opposite sides of an intersection, with a telltale trail of rocks and broken bottles littering the sidewalks. It had taken us a while to leave my grandmother's, since we wanted to make sure it was safe to get in the car and drive away without incident. The two groups, mainly young men, had been squabbling all afternoon, occasionally backing up their words by throwing something hard or sharp at the enemy, but when it seemed relatively peaceful, my dad had hustled us out of Grandma Jones's house and into the car.

We just wanted to get out of there and back to Turner's Station. And then we heard a loud *pop*.

"Get down!" Dad hollered, and we instantly made ourselves as small as we could in the backseat, convinced someone was shooting at us.

"What the heck . . . ?" he muttered, looking around frantically. Then he broke into a soft chuckle, and Mom joined in. Slowly we peeked over the seat to see what had happened.

No one had been trying to "get us." The "shot" we heard was the cork popping off a bottle of Cold Duck champagne, which had been rolling around under the front seat for weeks, maybe months— perhaps an overlooked New Year's Eve treat or gift that never made it out of the car and into the refrigerator. The bottle of bubbly, which had been shaking and baking in the car, picked that moment to blow its top.

The sound of my parents' laughter and the scent of spilled champagne reassured us as we rounded the corner, glad to leave the ugliness behind, for now.

IN MY JUNIOR year of high school, I auditioned for the school's spring musical for the very first time. After years of building my confidence performing as a puppeteer, I wanted to try going out onstage alone. My success as a local entertainer had all but pulled me out of my shell, and by the time I entered high school, I had grown more comfortable in front of other people.

True, there were still times when I wanted to stick my head inside a locker if some of the cool kids approached me, but for the most part I found my niche. I participated regularly in music and drama, had friends from the neighborhood as well as school pals, and so far, life was pretty good at Dundalk High School.

The neighborhood I grew up in was almost exclusively black, while the school drew from a wider geographic area—including the predominantly white community of Dundalk—and was much more racially diverse. By now, in the early and mid-1970s, most of the previous decade's racial unrest that had torn apart so many cities, including Baltimore, had quieted. Occasional rumblings still unsettled folks and tested nerves. At school, we had one incident where the police were called in that ultimately proved to be about drugs as well as race, but the media played up the racial angle and called a few kids squaring off in the cafeteria a riot.

Classes were canceled and school closed early. What I remember most about that incident is my drama teacher, Mr. Riggs, offering me a ride home so I wouldn't have to wait around for the bus. Mr. Riggs is white, and I'm black, but our skin color was never an issue. His act of kindness never made the news. The countless gestures of solidarity and generosity that were made throughout our community were also overlooked.

My mother and father always made sure we knew more about our hometown than the Baltimore City riots of 1968 and their aftermath. Turner Station has a long and proud history. In the 1880s, when the shipyards and steel mills were booming, Russian, Hungarian, and African American workers flocked to a nearby area called Sparrows Point. A mill town sprang up: white workers living on the south side, closest to the mill, and black workers on the north side. When white workers saved enough money to move out of mill housing, they headed across a fairly narrow inlet to what is today Dundalk. African American workers did not have that option because back then Dundalk was strictly segregated, for whites only.

For that reason, Turner Station grew up as its own community. Until then, blacks lived just outside Dundalk's city limits in a wooded area called The Meadows, while others gravitated to The Point. The Point, however, was actually located on property owned by the mill. No businesses were started there, in contrast to what eventually became Turner Station.

Turner's Station, as the locals came to call it, had plenty of commerce, owned, operated, and patronized by a growing community of working- and middle-class African American families. There were numerous grocery and drug stores, gasoline stations, beauty and barber shops, a savings and loan, clothing stores, a movie theater, and the Edgewater Amusement Park.

My mother and father were proud of the town, and in particular of two former residents: Kweisi Mfume, longtime radio personality, congressman, and one-time president of the NAACP, and Yale-educated Calvin Hill, who played professional football for the Dallas Cowboys and whose son, NBA superstar Grant Hill, gained national acclaim at Duke University. Turner's Station also produced more than its share of lawyers, doctors, and judges.

I'd like to think that, growing up in such a strong and proud community, I never experienced any overt racism, that it wouldn't creep into our little corner of the world. But when I decided to go to that audition for the spring musical at Dundalk High, I was about to get a close-up look at small-mindedness.

A pretty good singer, I won the role as the romantic lead Sky Masterson in *Guys and Dolls*, and I was floating on air. This was a dream role—to have some great acting scenes and perform show-stopping songs like "Luck Be a Lady," and "My Time of Day." I was also especially pleased that Sky's love interest, Sarah, was going to be played by a girl who was a friend of mine. She and I were in music and drama classes together, and she was bright and talented, with a remarkable voice. Getting a lead in a production was always a thrill, and I was riding high for days after the cast list was posted outside the music room.

A few days after we started rehearsals, I got a call from "Sarah." She started off talking about a bunch of different things, rambling and stumbling over her words, which I thought was odd. I could tell she was nervous and I didn't know what to make of it.

Eventually she got to the point. "You know, in the musical you and I have to kiss."

I said, "Yeah."

An awkward pause followed. I sensed what was coming next, but considering she was a friend, I wanted to give her the benefit of the doubt. I also wasn't about to make it any easier on her. I braced myself for what she was about to say.

"We can't do that."

What she was really saying was *We can't kiss in front of everyone at school because you are black and I am white.*

While I absorbed her comment, I could hear her mother in the background, clearly coaching her on what to say. Then my mom's radar went off because she overheard what I was saying to my friend, and she got involved. The four of us were all talking at once and then this girl delivered the line that really devastated me.

"Kevin, I think you should step down and quit the role of Sky Masterson."

I was stunned, but responded instantly and honestly. "What do you mean, *I* should *step down*? I don't have a problem with it. *You're* the one with the problem. I'm not going to quit—you should."

When my mom heard me repeat the words "step down," she went

off, pouring words into my ear. I could barely take in everything she was saying, but I knew that the fury in her was coming out.

My mom was socially aware and outspoken for her time, and I can best describe her beliefs by mentioning that we had a photo of Angela Davis prominently displayed in our home, right over the TV.

Davis's steely and defiant eyes stared down at me every time I sat in front of the living room television set, and it was difficult to ignore her and not reflect on her attitudes and beliefs. My mom's convictions developed naturally—her mother was known in her neighborhood for standing up to injustice and circulating petitions on various social issues. Neither my mother nor I was going to give up easily. Mom had taught me that there were times when I'd have to stand up for myself and what I truly believed in—to know what fights were worth engaging in. And this was shaping up to be one of those battles.

The conversation could have gone on and on, but I'd heard enough. "This is your problem," I told my friend. "You find a way to deal with it. I'm playing the role."

She eventually went to the director and gave up the choice part of Sarah, opting to sing and dance in the chorus instead. (Ironically, the role of Sarah was awarded to an equally talented classmate who happened to be African American. Turns out she had a crush on me, and she had no problem with the kiss scene.) Months later, "Sarah" apologized to me, and the two of us managed to get along. I know her mother had a lot to do with it, but I could never completely get over the assumption that because this girl was white I should "step down"—which really meant know my place.

Thankfully, this was an isolated incident, and my parents instilled in me the idea that right and wrong were neither black nor white. They have lived that simple ideal their whole lives, and from childhood I learned to appreciate the differences in people without sacrificing my identity.

I **DON'T THINK** it was any coincidence that, from my earliest days, I gravitated toward *Sesame Street*—first as a show to watch and admire and then as a place to foster my career. From its inception, *Sesame Street* has championed the cause of racial and ethnic diversity. The street itself and those who live on it—humans and puppets—are a mix of colors, races, and ethnic origins. In recent years, the human cast has been even more inclusive with differently abled children joining in the fun. Whether they are in a wheelchair or live with Down syndrome, have brown skin or blue fur, talk with an accent or don't talk much at all, everyone fits right in on *Sesame Street*.

Elmo, like most children, doesn't make snap judgments or subtle assumptions based on race, gender, or physical differences, and neither did Jim Henson, who welcomed diversity in the workplace before it was considered the norm. I spent almost fifteen years around him, and all of us—friends, family, and colleagues—agree that Jim was color-blind. When Jim would sing "It's Not Easy Being Green," it came straight from the heart.

Racism, or any kind of prejudice, is not an attitude that children are born with. It is a learned behavior, and children, unfortunately, are often subjected to it when they are most impressionable. It's all but impossible for young children or young adults to understand why prejudice exists in our free society, but before you know it, they've absorbed those attitudes. Undoing the damage can be difficult.

I remember that when I was a child, my mom grew upset when someone stared at us in a public place, as if we weren't supposed to be there (as if we were supposed to "step down"). Mom's anger stemmed from what she'd dealt with as a young child, watching her parents struggle against racist attitudes that were reinforced by legal segregation. I still remember seeing the riots on television—white people beating on black people—and feeling angry. It was a very confusing time to be a child; as kids, we were feeding off the anxieties of the adults around us and the images on TV, which brought the tensions right into our living rooms.

Elmo lovingly celebrates the differences between all people (and monsters), but he's still a little kid and, like any child, he can easily fall under the influence of others. One *Sesame Street* episode in particular drove that point home to me, and I hope we were successful in teaching kids an important lesson on tolerance.

The running theme centered on the story of the Big Bad Wolf and the Three Little Pigs. The show was "brought to you by the letter *U*," and Rosita built a large *U* out of blocks. Then the Big Bad Wolf comes along and blows it down. Rosita is upset that her letter *U* is ruined, but Elmo encourages her to rebuild it. With a little help from Elmo and the others, she puts the *U* back together. A few moments later, the Big Bad Wolf's cousin Leonard happens along.

No one wants him around—he's another wolf, after all—and they don't want to play with him or let him near the letter *U* for fear that he will blow it down, too. Leonard tries to explain that despite that fact he's a wolf, he's not like his cousin at all. With a sly bit of humor that adults will appreciate, Leonard goes so far as to explain that he's into tai chi, not huffing and puffing.

Elmo is among those who are initially skeptical, and he protests against Leonard's presence. But the group comes to see that Leonard is genuinely different from his cousin. He enthusiastically joins in the musical number "If You've Seen One Wolf, You've Not Seen Them All." Lesson learned, the Muppet cast laughs when, in their exuberance, they themselves knock the letter *U* down.

Another sketch modeled for children, in a metaphorical way, is a solution to intolerance. It didn't preach, but rather demonstrated to children, and reminded adults, that we are more the same than different.

In the sketch, Elmo wants to have a parade. He writes a song called "The Little Red Furry Monster Parade . . . *Hooray! Hooray!*" Elmo parades about, singing his song, when Zoe shows up and asks if she can join in. Elmo looks at her and says, "You're furry and little, but you're not red." Zoe replies, "Well, I would have loved to be in your parade, but I guess I can't be." Elmo thinks for a second and an-

nounces that he has a solution; he will change the song to "The Little Red, Furry and Orange Monster Day Parade."

Elmo and Zoe parade around singing, when Baby Bear shows up
and asks if he can join. Elmo says, "Well, you're furry, but you're not
a monster, you're a bear. And you're not orange or red." Baby Bear is
very disappointed and Elmo says, "Wait, wait, we can change the
song!" This cycle keeps repeating with each Muppet that comes
along, until it grows into a fifty-Muppet chorus.

Finally, Elmo says, "Why don't we just call it 'The Everybody Day
Parade!' " Nobody is left out of the parade. Every Muppet, like every
human being, is different. And the Muppets and their young audience learn that the best parades in life are composed of very different, very colorful individuals.

One of Elmo's guests in particular embodies the spirit of peace
and tolerance. Kofi Annan, the secretary-general of the United Nations, had asked to be on the show, and we were honored to have
him. He wanted to meet Elmo, and the two of them had a warm and
funny exchange. Annan had scheduled his appearance around his trip
to Stockholm to receive the Nobel Peace Prize, which intrigued
Elmo. The secretary-general behaved like a kind and patient grandfather, working in his message of peace while answering the kinds
of questions any three-and-a-half-year-old might have.

"Do you want to come and work with me at the United Nations
and make peace?" he asks.

"Oh, Elmo would love to. What would Elmo do?"

"I think I would take you on some of the peace negotiations, when people are fighting . . . to get them to make peace," Mr. Annan responds.

"Can Elmo wear a tie like that?"

"Well, yes, it will help," Mr. Annan says encouragingly.

As I spoke to Kofi Annan through Elmo, I thought of a child asking an important grown-up about his job. I focused on my performance, but a part of me was in awe of this man, who regularly deals with heads of state and with turmoil all over the globe. (We even talked about 9/11 and how scared Elmo was.) Yet despite his position of importance, Mr. Annan was gentle and calm, qualities that undoubtedly work for him on the job, as well.

In a very real sense, *Sesame Street* has its own form of the United Nations in its coproductions around the world. Mexico's *Plaza Sésamo* has been on the air for thirty-four years (and can be seen in this country on Spanish-language networks), and Abelardo (Big Bird's young cousin), Lola, and Pancho are as familiar to Latin American children as Elmo, Grover, and the rest of the U.S. cast are to children here.

In one of the most troubled areas in the world, Sesame Productions and a team from Jordan, Israel, and Palestine developed "Sesame Stories" to promote understanding and goodwill among children in that region and address the specific cultural and linguistic needs of children there. (Currently, each country has its own production.)

Sometimes I think that well-intentioned people believe the notion of diversity involves treating everyone equally. At *Sesame Street*, we try to model celebrating what makes us different and unique as people and cultures. That isn't always easy for us to remember as we consult on and oversee some of these international productions. I was a small but proud contributor to Sesame International's initiative in South Africa, where this issue surfaced.

I worked in South Africa auditioning puppeteers. While apartheid had officially ended, it was clear that remnants of the official policy remained, but the people we worked with and others I came in contact with were inspiring and amazingly hopeful about the future.

The folks at *Takalani Sesame* were wonderful and also wonderfully aggressive in remaining committed to creating material to address the many needs of young people growing up in the shadow of apartheid and the AIDS epidemic devastating many parts of Africa. Though those of us in the United States were uncertain at first if it was the right thing to do, their passionate advocacy of their cause convinced us that they had to educate children about the disease.

To do so, *Takalani Sesame* created a character named Kami who was infected with the virus from her now-deceased mother. Pretty heavy stuff for a children's show, but when you hear of the staggering numbers of dying African men, women, and children, and the horrible lack of education and misinformation and folklore plaguing health authorities' efforts to stem the tide, you understand how important and how necessary this character and story line are for South Africa's future.

Kami is a little girl monster Muppet, and she has no outward signs of the disease. Both these facts help to soften the message from a more factual documentary approach to the kind of teaching and learning *Sesame Street* is so well known for. The other characters are curious about her condition and ask her why she doesn't seem sick, and Kami offers an explanation typical of what a young child would know and be able to express.

In one incredibly moving segment, Kami brings out her "memory box" to show everyone. In parts of Africa where AIDS is rampant (the UN estimates that AIDS has orphaned more than 13 million children in sub-Saharan Africa), the practice of creating a memory box, where people can preserve items that remind them of a loved one who is dying or has died of the disease, is increasingly common. Experts on grieving advocate this practice as emotionally healthy and necessary, particularly among young children who are losing one or both parents to AIDS.

Inside the box, Kami has her mother's passport, a scarf her mother wore that carries her lingering scent, and photographs of the two of them together. She shares her memories of her mother, an important part of dealing with loss. In a really heartfelt and funny *Sesame Street* touch, one of the other characters, Zekewe, decides to create his own memory box, which he shares with Kami.

Zekewe is an older character who once drove a taxi that now sits on the set on cinder blocks in complete disrepair. His memory box is filled with parts of the car that once worked, and he has fond and funny memories of each. In a way Jim Henson would have appreciated, the humor in the piece helped to balance the sadness of Kami's loss and created a sensitive and educational show about a very difficult issue.

Despite the company's initial hesitation and uncertainty about presenting children with issues like AIDS and the death of a parent, they had to let go of their preconception of what was right for the kids of South Africa and acknowledge the very real differences between our cultures.

Though the issues faced by American and South African children seem worlds apart, our goal was the same: to teach tolerance. Unfortunately, some very narrow-minded Americans who had never seen the episodes tried to prevent us from teaching that lesson. Although the *Takalani Sesame* episodes were produced and intended solely for use in South Africa, when a conservative U.S. organization heard that a *Sesame Street* production was using a character with AIDS and dealing with that subject matter, its members raised a stink. Why? Because we receive government funding, as does PBS, and we were raising the hot-button issue of HIV/AIDS. In their eyes, we were somehow pushing the "gay agenda," which they saw as an objectionable bias. (The PBS program *Postcards from Buster* came under similar fire when it featured some children being raised by same-sex parents.) When I returned from South Africa, even the security people at the airport commented on the inappropriateness of an HIV/AIDS plotline on a children's television show; they just didn't get it.

To me, these objections were sad and outrageously disrespectful, and like many prejudicial attitudes, were born out of intolerance and ignorance. HIV/AIDS doesn't discriminate based on sexual preference. In Africa, it has destroyed the lives of countless heterosexual married couples and their families.

I don't know how anyone who saw Kami and her memory box could have raised a single objection to the show's content or the South African production company's handling of the material. Although we have come so far in learning and teaching tolerance, we still have a long way to go. I salute *Takalani Sesame* for their courage in taking on the subject and for their sensitive and inspiring handling of the issue. I'm glad that we at the Sesame Workshop could help to make it happen.

ELMO LOVES HIS red fur," Elmo tells Whoopi Goldberg in a sketch they did together. They are sitting close together on a bench, and Elmo is comparing his appearance to Whoopi's.

"I love my brown skin," Whoopi replies. She touches his red fur and tickles him, and Elmo touches her dreads.

Like many children, Elmo is curious about the differences between himself and the new people he meets. When Whoopi Goldberg visited *Sesame Street*, it was a perfect opportunity for Elmo to investigate the miraculous variety of skin color (or fur color, as the case may be).

Raised by a single mother in lower Manhattan, Whoopi had a

number of jobs before she hit it big. In a funny twist, she worked as a babysitter for a woman whose children auditioned for and regularly appeared on *Sesame Street*, and she regularly ferried them to and from the set. When I look at Whoopi, I see a woman who is still actively involved in getting children where they need to be.

Whoopi will tell you that she is a big fan of Elmo and a friend of *Sesame Street* for a number of reasons, but chief among them is her shared desire to foster self-esteem in young people. She has made a career out of celebrating individuality, and though she may not be secretary-general of the United Nations, she's just as much a symbol of diversity and tolerance as Kofi Annan.

In their scene on the bench, Whoopi and Elmo are modeling self-esteem. If children are not taught to value themselves, then they will not value others. And if they don't learn to respect each other, then those damaging assumptions about things like race and gender and religion will begin to blur their vision of the world.

I STILL REMEMBER peering out my Grandmother Jones's front window that day in 1968, one hand holding back the sun-faded white lace curtains. In the other, I held the usual come-visiting treat she offered—one of her heavenly sweet biscuits, slathered with salty butter.

Only now do I realize how appropriate that combination was—the sweet goodness of life in a country where we've made so many strides, the salty tears that have been shed over struggles of race and class. But people like Whoopi, like Kofi Annan, like the teacher who gave me a ride home, like Jim Henson, or like my own parents, who taught me to be proud of where I was from and who I was, give me hope that despite our differences, there is plenty of room in this big, wide world for all of us to live together in peace.

5

COURAGE

MY FRIEND CINDY was about my age at the time, sixteen. She walked on weak, shaky legs to the piano at the center of the stage, where everyone in the audience could see what the chemotherapy had done to her once-vibrant beauty. She had no hair, she had no color in her cheeks, and she had no time to be sad. But she still possessed a brilliant light in her eyes and a heavenly voice to match. Cindy Dosch, who would stay on this earth for only two more months, sat down to play and sing, to give us one final gift. And that, to me, was courage.

CALL IT BRAVERY, call it guts, call it sheer will, or call it courage. It's the Cowardly Lion, who travels to Oz and finally gets his nerve back; the firefighters charging into burning buildings on search and rescue missions; people all over the world who sacrifice their lives standing up to Goliath-like injustice; the victims of natural disasters, who pick up the pieces and start over after their devastating losses. For Cindy, courage simply meant holding fast to something that she loved—music, the stage, the act of entertaining others—even as her life slipped away.

I met Cindy through the high school drama productions and musicals I took part in, a colorful and exciting world I quickly embraced. I loved the adrenaline-filled auditions, the grind of rehearsals, the pleasures of walking the empty and darkened school hallways when we were done, long after everyone else had gone home. At times like that, the school felt like my private domain.

Cindy was a veteran of these productions, with a gorgeous, powerful soprano that rocked her just-shy-of-five-foot frame. How such a wave of sound came out of such a small body was a marvel. Cindy and I starred together in *Oliver!* (she as the title character and me as Fagin) and in *You're a Good Man, Charlie Brown*. She was as saucy and bossy a Lucy as ever inhabited the role.

Offstage, she was anything but Lucy-like. She was one of the kindest, gentlest, and most soulful young women I've ever met. Her rich, warm laugh was as beautiful as her singing voice. Over time, we became good friends with a shared passion for theater and performance.

Besides school plays, we also worked together often, one time appearing at the Waxter Center—an elder care facility where she wowed everyone with her rendition of "I Nearly Missed a Rainbow," a *Sesame Street* tune from the 1970s. At sixteen, her interpretation was so pitch perfect that I knew her name would be up in lights someday. One day shortly after the Waxter Center event, I saw her standing in the hallway frowning.

"What's up, Miss Cindy? Everything all right?" I asked her. I sometimes commented on how serious she was, how she walked around a lot of the time as if she were deep in thought. She chewed at her bottom lip for a moment. "Everything's okay. Just thinking about some things at home that I have to fix." She walked off with a quick wave.

Cindy frequently complained of headaches, and by the middle of our junior year, they became so persistent and so debilitating that she had to see a doctor. She received the worst possible diagnosis: cancer.

I was shocked when I learned the news. I had to do something to help Cindy, but I felt powerless. Then I came up with a plan. I could show everyone how talented she was and give her one last chance to perform for an audience.

I had been doing puppet shows in and around Baltimore for a while now and had even started appearing on a local children's television show hosted by Stu Kerr, my friend and mentor. I invited Cindy to sing with me at a show Stu and I were doing at the Inner Harbor, Baltimore's waterfront shopping and entertainment complex. She eagerly agreed. She sang "Corner of the Sky" from the musical *Pippin* to my puppet Bartee. Chemotherapy had taken her hair, and her delicate features were nearly lost in the puffiness of her face. Her rendition brought the house down and tears to my eyes. She died eight weeks later.

Even though I knew for some time that her death was inevitable, I was devastated when I found out. I went into the choral classroom and sat on the piano bench and stared at her seat for a few minutes. I couldn't imagine that she wasn't going to barrel into the room as she usually did, arms loaded with books, her voice and presence lighting up the room. I expressed my grief and love for Cindy through my craft, and at her funeral, I gave her mother a clown puppet to donate to a children's cancer charity in Cindy's name.

One thing I learned back then was that performing in front of an audience made me step outside of myself and forget for a little while whatever was troubling me. I'll always remember Cindy's final performance with me, and the courage she displayed. She was so thin and frail, I thought she wouldn't get through the song, but when we got out on that stage, that voice . . . Lord, that voice.

Her eyes shone and her rapturous voice washed out across the audience all the way to the back rows. She made it seem effortless. Cindy had the guts to live her last days with passion, sharing her gift and getting out in front of an audience to do what she loved.

FOR SUCH A small monster, Elmo has an enormously brave heart. He's taught me so much about courage, especially about staying strong in the face of painful circumstances.

As part of my work with *Sesame Street*, my fellow Muppeteers and I regularly visit and entertain sick children. Working with organizations like the Make-A-Wish Foundation, we go into hospitals and visit with kids, parents, and medical staff, or sometimes invite the children onto the set of the show. Doing this type of performance is as rewarding as it is challenging. But I admit I found it particularly difficult when I first started doing the work, until I let Elmo take over.

I found it hard to move past the emotional hurdles, especially if we were working with terminally ill children. I'd look at their parents, I'd think of my own daughter, and I'd feel incredibly sad. But then I'd remember: My job was to entertain, and it was time to let Elmo do his thing.

Elmo knows how to see a child and not a disease or a condition. What Elmo sees is a potential playmate, someone who wants to laugh and sing and have fun with him like all his other friends do. Once a beautiful little girl was brought to the set in a wheelchair. I could read the pain behind the smiles of her parents when they thanked us for granting this last wish. Despite the lights and action on the set, their daughter's eyes were closed and she didn't speak or move.

I brought Elmo up to her, and at first I didn't know what to do since she wasn't looking at us. Elmo took over. He knew that she could hear him, and he wanted a hug and wanted to give her one, as well, so he snuggled up close to her and started whispering the words to the song "Sing." Gradually his voice grew stronger as he saw the beginnings of an uncertain smile at the corner of her mouth. Her smile gained confidence as Elmo's voice rose.

It took every bit of control I had to keep going. I focused on Elmo and his new friend: two little kids who just want to sing and have fun. Thoughts of what those parents had been through, were going through, and were soon to face gave me strength. Certainly I could summon a fraction of their courage and sing that song.

I WAS WAITING for the principal of Baltimore's Battle Monument School, a learning center for children facing physical, mental, and/or emotional challenges. I was still in high school myself and hadn't had much experience yet dealing with kids like this, but I was there to entertain the kids. Little did I know that I was also there to learn some lessons.

The door opened and out came principal Charles Mayer, his shuffling gait supported with a cane. His appearance surprised me, but he moved easily enough and shook my hand with a strong grip as he smiled ferociously.

"I'm so glad you're here! Let me show you around before we get started." He led me from his office and down the hallway, mixing personal greetings to everyone he encountered with an explanation of the school's philosophy, which centered on teaching the students to be as self-sufficient as possible.

When I saw a student struggling to balance his books and turn the knob on the water fountain, I automatically took a step toward him to help, but Mr. Mayer stopped me with a viselike grip on my right arm.

"Mr. Clash, that's kind of you, but we only assist our students when it's absolutely necessary, especially with everyday tasks. We want them to depend on themselves, not on others."

During my performance, I did a lot of interacting with the audience, and Mr. Mayer was one of the most enthusiastic participants. He had a hearty laugh, more like a roar, that practically shook the whole auditorium. At times I wasn't sure if the kids were enjoying watching me as much as I enjoyed watching Mr. Mayer and them.

After my puppet show, I was placing Bartee and a couple of other puppets into a case when I heard Mr. Mayer ask for everyone's attention. While I'd been packing, the custodial staff had brought out two sets of risers, which I assumed were for a later event. The auditorium was still abuzz with postshow chatter, and no one made any attempt to leave. Mr. Mayer asked for everyone's attention.

"By way of thanking our guest performer, we would like to present the Battle Monument School choir." I looked around for the rest of the audience, but I seemed to be it!

Given the children's various levels of disability, it took a few moments for them to gather on the risers and for those in wheelchairs to get positioned on the stage. Once the first sure notes of the piano started, I forgot all about their challenges as the choir serenaded me with two songs. The joyful noise of music soothed and elated me, and I was touched. I also felt a deep appreciation of the courage these children summoned to go about their daily tasks, to carry on with their lives, and to get up on a stage and sing for me.

These students didn't just show me gratitude with their performance; they shared with me their spirit and dedication, and reminded me that difficult challenges can be handled with grace and humor.

In part inspired by Mr. Mayer's students, I decided to organize a fund-raising variety show called "A Night to Remember" to benefit the Muscular Dystrophy Association. The organization's annual Labor Day telethon was a can't-miss opportunity to see some of my favorite stars and stay up well past my bedtime to see the tote board roll over. I wanted our contribution to help those digits turn.

We used the auditorium at Dundalk High School for the event, and our drama teacher, Mr. Riggs (the same Mr. Riggs who gave me that ride home), and our music teacher, Mr. Miller, assisted us. The night was a big success, and we brought in nearly three hundred dollars in ticket sales and pass-the-hat contributions. The following Monday, I was in my study hall, still feeling that postshow high, when a student aide walked in. Instead of going to the monitor as aides usually did, she made her way over to me. She said hello and handed me a hall pass. "The principal would like to see you."

I took the pass and looked it over. Sure enough, the principal had summoned me. I smiled. I thought that maybe he wanted to make a donation or thank me for supporting such a worthy cause. When I reached his office, his secretary nodded toward an empty seat just outside his closed door.

A few minutes' wait gave me more time to speculate on how generously he would thank me, until the secretary told me that I could go in. The principal sat behind a big mahogany desk, far different from the blocky teachers' desks. He didn't tell me to sit down, didn't offer his hand, he just sat there shuffling papers and squinting.

"Well, Mr. Clash. It seems we have a . . . problem," he finally began.

My stomach felt queasy and my heart started to pound as I wondered what I'd done wrong.

"I understand you used our auditorium on Saturday night. Since that was not a school-sponsored event, you have to pay for the use of the auditorium, as well as the lighting equipment and the sound system. So I'm afraid I'm going to have to take whatever money you brought in for the evening."

So many thoughts were spinning through my head. I'd never really been in trouble before, so being summoned to the principal's office was disorienting to begin with. I'd been expecting to be thanked, not reprimanded.

"Sir, we had permission. We were raising money for MDA."

"You may have had permission from your drama and music teachers, but you did not have the school board's authorization. According to school district policy, any use of the taxpayers' facilities must be approved in advance . . ." He went on and on with a bunch of other bureaucratic bull. After a few seconds, all I heard was the voice used for any parent or teacher on the *Peanuts* television specials: "Wah-WHA-wah-wah-wah-wha . . ."

Normally, I would have just stood there meekly. I was raised to have nothing but respect for authority figures, but this situation was ridiculous.

"Sir, this is not fair. You can't take money from a charity." I tried every other tactic I could think of, but he would not relent. We had to turn over the money. The principal kept insisting that he had a responsibility to uphold the policies of the school board. Sometimes you learn a lot about courage when you see its opposite in action. I was not proud of this school, and when it came time to purchase my class ring, I wouldn't buy one.

PEOPLE OFTEN ASK if I ever get nervous when I perform, or if I ever had stage fright. I guess I did, at one time, but after all these years, I've developed my own kind of courage—I just get out there and do it! But I still worry about flopping. Though Elmo proved to be a hit, not everything I've tried on *Sesame Street* has succeeded.

For every Elmo in my past, there's been a Ferlinghetti Donizetti, the rhyming beatnik who just didn't quite catch on, or a Professor D. Rabbit, whose shtick was so bad that I don't even remember it. But these Muppet also-rans don't stop us from trying out new things and taking creative risks. While these acts may not require the same kind of level of courage it takes to get through life's truly challenging moments, they do require a form of get-your-butt-out-there-and-give-it-a-shot courage that all of us draw on every day.

Let's see . . . there was the Grand High Triangle Lover Muppet, who loved triangles, obviously, and who had a personality modeled on Ralph Cramden. He even had an Ed Norton–like sidekick who would hit a triangle and announce the presence of the exalted one: "Make way for the Grand High Triangle Lover!" My character would turn to his sidekick, and in my best effort at channeling the Jackie Gleason magic, he'd say, "WILL YOU CUT THAT OUT?" Kids didn't get the whole *Honeymooners'* thing, and after a while, we dropped it.

And of course, there was Juggles the Juggler, perhaps our most spectacular failure. I puppeteered the head of the character and we found a talented performance artist named Fred Garbo to do the juggling while squatting just under the camera's frame. Talk about tough! Trying to coordinate my actions with Fred's was next to impossible. Fred was the best, but this was asking too much. We spent most of our time in rehearsal rounding up dropped balls, stumbling over one another, and flubbing lines of dialogue—just try concentrating on what you're saying when you've got balls flying around your head.

Knowing when to admit you're in over your head takes courage. I played nine characters on *Sesame Street* at one time or another, and three—Elmo, Hoots the Owl, and Natasha—were successful. A .333 batting average is great in baseball and pretty good in puppetry.

I learned a lot from flopping—that overly ambitious acts like Juggles were hard to pull off, that some characters just didn't click with us or the viewers no matter how clever they were (perhaps too clever), and that maybe *The Honeymooners* is an acquired taste. Most of all, I learned that you can't be afraid to fail, because you never know true success unless you have a flop or two (or six).

BECAUSE SESAME STREET is filmed in New York (just across the East River at Kaufman Astoria Studios in Queens), we all felt the impact of the events of September 11, 2001. In those surreal days following the attacks, we sought solace with one another amid the constant reminders—on television, on street corners, and in subway stations where "Have You Seen?" notices flapped like prayer flags. We struggled ourselves to regain some semblance of normalcy while fighter jets circled and the rubble of what was once our lives smoldered.

We also knew that children everywhere, not just in New York and Washington, were profoundly affected by those terrible days. No matter how hard we tried to protect our children, the images in the papers and on TV were unrelenting, and the grown-up conversation swirling around young ears inevitably would drift to the nightmarish scenarios that had become all too real.

At *Sesame Street*, the producers quickly decided we needed to do something to help kids come to terms with the loss—whether it was the loss of a loved one or a loss of innocence. The writers, producers, director, and cast created several new episodes to model behaviors that could make a real and immediate difference in the lives of children.

One episode dealt with Elmo and his fearful reaction to a fire. As adults we understand how heroic firefighters are, and 9/11 brought that message home intensely. But though kids are taught that firefighters are brave and helpful, many are afraid of the men and women who might one day save their lives. In a chaotic situation like a fire, with rescuers dressed in bulky outfits and wearing monstrous-looking oxygen masks that hide their faces, children have been known to hide or run away.

Elmo was having lunch in Mr. Hooper's store with Maria. Alan (played by Alan Muraoka), who runs the store, was cooking fried chicken in the kitchen when a grease fire broke out. The cast modeled fire safety strategies, with Elmo and Maria (played by Sonia Manzano) staying low, and getting out of the building.

Both in the studio and on location, we used real New York City firefighters, many of whom were just months removed from having lost brothers and sisters in the department. Despite their enormous suffering, they were glad for the diversion as well as the role they played in reassuring Elmo, and our children, that despite their potentially frightening-looking helmets, masks, and other gear, they are there to help us, not hurt us. By learning as much as he could about the role of firefighters and their life-saving equipment, Elmo was able to get over his fear.

After I performed that sketch, some friends and colleagues told me that Elmo's fear seemed especially palpable. The fact is that I, like so many people around me, was feeling some very real fear and tension myself after 9/11, and I was able to channel that emotion into my performance. Maybe it would have been easier just to carry on with the business of entertaining kids and teaching them lessons from our regular curriculum, but at *Sesame Street*, we saw an opportunity to perform a service for children and their parents by transforming something horrible into something positive.

After 9/11, we traveled to various schools around the city, met with young children who'd lost parents or who'd been displaced from their homes and their schools. Many of them were struggling to deal with a bewildering set of circumstances, made even more difficult by the fact that their parents were trying to cope with their own conflicting feelings. I know that Genia and I found ourselves treading water assisting Shannon as her fears for my safety in New York and the proximity of her own home to Washington, D.C., nearly swamped her.

The enormous loss of life was too difficult a subject for us to deal with directly, and the wounds were too fresh, but we did craft a show around loss: Big Bird adopts a wild pet turtle, who wanders off. Everyone on the street helps him to cope. Demonstrating the kind of courage we all need in the face of loss, Big Bird rallies and thanks his many friends for their support.

We also created two shows to deal with a serious side effect of 9/11—bullying and cultural diversity. Even in a time of crisis, when not many of our political leaders were championing the message of tolerance, *Sesame Street* rose to the occasion and bravely faced a difficult but important topic—and one that has been central to the show from its inception.

OFTEN IT IS harder to find the courage to face a personal difficulty than it is to understand and accept a large-scale tragedy. After many years together, and a lot of time apart, Genia and I finally admitted that our relationship was in trouble. We love each other deeply, but after seventeen years, it was not enough to sustain our marriage. We struggled for a long time over the impact that our separation and eventual divorce would have on our daughter.

Few children can emerge unscathed from the impact of divorce. (In fact, we filmed—but never aired—a *Sesame Street* sketch dealing with divorce; the test audience of kids found it too unsettling and confusing, despite how carefully our research department and curriculum writers structured the segment. The kids, not all of them children of divorce, couldn't get past the idea of losing a parent.) Like many couples, Genia and I didn't want our child to get caught in the middle.

I know that "courage" is a difficult word for some to associate with divorce, but making a difficult decision, weighing the effects of that choice on a number of other people, and following through was not easy for either of us. Though we both ached inside, we were more worried about our child than ourselves. Summoning up as much courage as we could, Genia and I sat Shannon down and explained to her what was happening and what she could expect.

6

FRIENDSHIP

LHM'06

THE COIL OF rope was so thick that I imagined it had once been used to moor a gigantic ship down in Baltimore Harbor. It had that strong hemp smell, and it felt powerful and heavy in my small hands. Dad would never miss it. I hauled that rope out of the shed and carried it across the lawn.

You would have thought I was the Pied Piper of Hamelin the way my neighborhood friends followed me, asking me what I was doing. I was a little master showman, so I simply shrugged and said, "You'll see." (I didn't always know myself.) It was a picture-perfect summer day, and we were taking a break from chores to goof around outside, but baseball or tag was a bit too tame. I didn't want to just play with my friends. I wanted to do something different; I wanted to *entertain* them.

Once there was a time, for all of us, when making friends was as easy and natural as breathing, even for someone shy like me. I never lacked for company when it came to other kids, and I had three friends in particular—Richard Green, Lorraine McCullough, and Orlando Jackson—whom I played with constantly. (My mom took care of a number of them, so I got to see them daily.) In my own quiet way, I was becoming the neighborhood ringleader, and Richard, Lorraine, and Orlando were always ready to go along with me when I had a plan.

I sent them into the field by our house to harvest the thick-as-hay grass the county had cut down and left behind. Every few minutes, one of them would return carrying an armful, nose twitching from the dusty load. Following my orders, they dumped the grass in a pile beneath the huge oak tree in the field until we had a nice high mound. Now we were really grabbing the attention of the neighborhood kids. Next I took a rectangular foot-long piece of lumber I'd scavenged and notched out the corners, parading into the field as my audience watched and wondered.

I shinnied up the tree with the coil of rope and looped one end over an enormous branch. Once back on the ground, I helped Orlando tie some knots in the other end to attach the rope to our makeshift seat.

Richard went first. While he sat on the seat, Orlando, Lorraine, and I hauled on the other end of the rope, pulley style, and lifted him until his head was just about level with the branch, a good eight feet or more. To the appreciative oohs and ahhs of the crowd, we let go of the rope and Richard tumbled gleefully into the pile. Of course, everyone wanted a turn, and we happily hauled one another skyward. (The lighter you were, the higher you went.) As the grass collected on our pants and in our hair, our cushiony landing pad began to flatten out. Too wrapped up in the pleasure of it all, we didn't take the time to replenish the stock of grass. Then someone went down hard and went home crying.

That ended the high-wire act for the day—and for the rest of the summer, once our mothers heard through the grapevine what had gone on. Richard, Orlando, Lorraine, and I had been identified as the perpetrators of the enterprise that had resulted in the injury. (Actually, the kid only had the wind knocked out of him and was more scared than hurt.) Our mothers wanted to know whose bright idea it was to create this primitive and ill-conceived bungee jump, and without consulting with one another, we all came up with the same answer: "I don't know." Kevin didn't know. Orlando didn't know. Lorraine didn't know. Richard didn't know.

Your blood-related brothers and sisters will almost always rat you out, but childhood friends practice a strict code of loyalty: They'll never tell.

TO ELMO, AND to many other children, friends are deeply important. Elmo is always so happy to see Zoe, Baby Bear, Big Bird, or any friend he happens to encounter. He looks at each meeting as an opportunity for fun. On "Elmo's World," in particular, he offers an enthusiastic greeting to his goldfish Dorothy, to Mr. Noodle, to Mr. Noodle's brother Mr. Noodle, to his door, his television, his computer, even to his stubborn window shades.

In person, of course, Elmo behaves the same way, offering up hugs and kisses to anyone who wants them. Children behave likewise, greeting each other and the grown-ups in their lives with warmth and affection. When a child says hello with such genuine feeling, it's impossible not to feel welcome. Kids seem to know instinctively that friendship is something to seek out and celebrate.

Adults, however, tend to "celebrate" in a more quiet and dignified manner, with a handshake and greetings like "Nice to see you," or "Hi, how are you?" (which we rattle off without expecting a truthful answer). Somewhere along the path to adulthood, we shift gears when it comes to making friends. We become more selective and discriminating. We worry about the cool kids and the cliques that didn't exist the year before. We may try to hang on to a few old childhood pals, but we change schools, move away from home, our interests shift, we find ourselves with a different group of people in a new city. We have "office friends."

Most of all, we get consumed by the real world and don't have as much time to nurture our friendships as we once did. Our personal relationships with others inevitably shift and change as our lives take shape, but I often think it would be wonderful to hang on to that gutsy, give-it-your-all style of friendship that Elmo and his youngest fans embrace.

WHEN I WAS thirteen, I glimpsed the shifting nature of friendship, when I faced a tough situation that tested my willingness to hold my tongue, to "not tell" on my friends.

By the time I was a teenager, I was considered the Richie Cunningham of the neighborhood: the squeaky-clean kid who never got into trouble—though I wasn't trying to be a Goody Two-shoes. The reality is that I wasn't a follower. It wasn't in my personality. I had no real interest in drinking or smoking or doing drugs even when others around me were experimenting. When I had appendicitis as a teenager, the doctor asked, "Do you drink?" I said no. "Do you smoke?" "No." "Have you had sex?" "No." "What are you, a damn angel?" she said. I most definitely was not an angel, but I did believe in doing my own thing.

By now, Orlando and his family had moved out of Turner's Station, to a more upscale community about forty minutes away. When he invited me for an overnight visit, I took two buses to get there. By the time I arrived at Orlando's, his parents had gone out for the afternoon, and a few of his new friends from the area had come over.

We were just hanging out in the basement rec room. There was a turntable and the guys asked me to be the DJ. Music was my thing and I gladly obliged, crashing on a bean bag chair in between sets by the Jackson Five and the Silvers. After a while, when I roused myself to get up to change the album again, I realized they must have gone upstairs because I was all alone. I headed for the kitchen, leaving Tom Jones singing "It's Not Unusual."

They weren't just eating; they were drinking. The guys had gotten their hands on a bottle of wine, some beer, and a bottle of vodka and some mixers. Orlando looked at me and twitched an eyebrow. He knew better than to offer me liquor. The four boys proceeded to get drunk while I watched from the sidelines, going back downstairs to change the music that no one else seemed to be listening to.

Within an hour, they were wasted, and I was still stone-cold sober. "Orlando, man," I said, feeling like I had to step in. "You guys should stop." I tried a few times to get through to him, but he was caught up in the moment.

At first I was thinking more about what would happen when his parents found out the liquor was missing, but they were acting crazier and crazier. They started dueling with the cue sticks, but then they decided to take the party outside by the swimming pool. I'd grown up on the Chesapeake and knew that drunk or sober, the water's edge was no place to mess around. (My classmate Skylow would later drown in the bay along with another friend when they tried to swim in the strong tides.) "You guys ought to cool it," I prodded, genuinely concerned about their safety, but they wouldn't listen. Fortunately, the buzz didn't last long before they were crashing. No one got hurt, but I was afraid. Back in the neighborhood, I'd seen what alcohol could do to people, and I knew it started early.

Orlando and I didn't talk about what had happened that night. I spent most of my time cleaning up the mess the guys had made so that things wouldn't look so bad when his parents came home. I knew I had to tell my mom what happened. I was worried about Orlando, and didn't like the changes I saw.

"Kevin, you've got to tell Mr. and Mrs. Jackson." As I've mentioned, my mom had babysat Orlando for years. If he was a friend to me, he was like a son to her.

I looked at her, my eyes bugging. She wore her "I told you once and I'm not going to tell you again" face. I knew on one level she was right—we were lucky nothing really bad happened. I wanted to be loyal to Orlando, and I didn't want to see him get into trouble with his parents. But I thought about where this could lead, and I didn't want to see him get into a more serious kind of trouble down the road.

The phone felt sweaty in my hand as I picked up the receiver to dial. His mother, whom we called Miss Hattie, answered and listened as I told the whole story. Orlando's dad, Mr. Melvin, was right beside her, listening in, both of them "umh-hmming" at every key point in the story.

"Orlando," said Mr. Melvin. "Is that what happened?"

Apparently Orlando was on the other extension.

Without a moment's hesitation, my friend said, "No."

At first I couldn't believe it, but before I could think about Orlando's response, his mom quickly thanked me and hung up.

When I went to school that Monday, I found out that Orlando had been punished. No one would speak to me. Lorraine, Richard, and other friends of Orlando's were giving me the silent treatment since I'd broken the kid code by telling his parents. But we weren't kids anymore. I was being Orlando's friend, but maybe not in the way he wanted me to. Eventually it all blew over, though I doubt anyone understood how hard it had been for me to rat out a friend and make that call.

It had been easier to be friends when we were little, when we could spill out the back door and into the yard to play kickball, or chase each other endlessly with no real goal, or sit in companionable silence in front of the TV while we watched cartoons. But true friends make an effort to stick together, even as it gets harder, even as they move in opposite directions.

Thirty years later, and thousands of miles apart, Orlando and I are still brothers.

WHEREVER YOU LOOK on *Sesame Street*, you'll see friendship in action, whether it's human characters interacting with each other, modeling respect and kindness, or not-exactly-human characters behaving like loyal, true companions. (What better example of a lasting friendship than that of Bert and Ernie?) But just as in the real world, friendships are often tested.

For a long time, no one on the street believed that Big Bird had a real friend named Snuffleupagus. They believed that Big Bird *believed* he was real, but that was as far as they were willing to go. Elmo, however, trusted Big Bird thoroughly. If Big Bird believed Snuffy was real, then Elmo believed it, too. He put his faith in his feathered friend.

Big Bird was disappointed that all his other friends hadn't believed him, but he rewarded Elmo's trust by convincing Snuffy to stay with Elmo. Big Bird wanted the others to see Snuffy, so he entrusted Elmo with an important task—to hold on to Snuffy's snuffle to make sure he didn't leave before Big Bird could round up everyone for the unveiling. Elmo didn't let his friend down; he held tight to that snuffle until everyone came by. The doubting Thomases had their eyes opened.

Though we may not make friends as effortlessly as children do, as adults we still look for qualities like loyalty and trust. I was lucky enough to find those qualities, and so many more, in my boss, Jim Henson. While our relationship began as a professional one, in time it deepened into something more profound. Jim was indeed "the boss of all Muppets," but he was, most of all, a true friend to everyone who worked for him.

We met when I did the Macy's Thanksgiving Day Parade for the very first time. There was an after-party for parade participants at Macy's, and I walked in alongside Diana Ross and Herb Alpert: two huge celebrities and the kid from Turner's Station. Photographers were snapping away and fans were shouting at them, and at me—like I was a star! Once inside, I stood alone taking in the scene, until Kermit Love came over to speak to me. As he was talking, I saw Jim Henson—a man I'd idolized for years—on the other side of the room. Forget Diana and Herb—there was Jim Henson! Kermit wanted to introduce me to Jim, and the thought of that all but robbed me of speech as we made our way over to where he stood.

I could barely say my own name, but Jim was warm and gracious, thanking me for having helped out on the float. He instantly put me at ease (though it took me two weeks to get over the excitement of meeting him). Over the years, I've met and worked with a lot of famous people, and most of them are surprisingly down to earth and attentive, but there was something special about the way Jim held my gaze. I immediately felt like I could trust this person, who seemed to have a gift for focusing his attention so that I felt genuinely valued.

Eventually I would go to work for Jim, and over the years I watched as he somehow maintained control yet never behaved like "the boss." In part, it was because Jim—an industry giant, a savvy businessperson, a creative genius—still got down and dirty with the rest us by Muppeteering.

During the shooting of the Muppets' twentieth-anniversary special in 1985, Jim placed Steve Whitmire, my colleague, and me in charge of the other puppeteers. In one ensemble scene, a production number, a group of rabbit Muppets danced in a highly choreographed group like the Rockettes. I was watching a rehearsal on the monitor, so all I could see was what viewers would eventually see: a group of rabbits. I couldn't see the puppeteers even when I watched the action live because of the set in front of them.

I thought that we must have somebody really raw doing one of the rabbits. Every other rabbit but this one was in step, and he wasn't just out of sync with the others, he was flailing around as joyfully as any character I'd ever seen.

I walked over to the floor manager, Wayne Moss, and said, "Listen, we've got to do something about that one rabbit. He's all over the place. Please tell whoever it is to get it together with the others."

Wayne pulled his headset off of one ear and looked at me quizzically. "Are you sure you want me to pass that message along?"

I told him yes, fully expecting he would walk over to the offending rabbit and straighten him out personally. Instead, he shrugged, tugged his headset back on, pulled his microphone toward him, and spoke into it. I wondered why Wayne was talking on the headset instead of doing what I'd asked him. Jim had specifically asked Steve and me to check out the puppeteering and make sure this scene looked good, and I wasn't about to disappoint him.

I was getting ready to tell Wayne that I would speak to the misguided rabbit myself if that would help things, when the rabbit in question dropped down out of the group. A moment later, Jim's bearded face popped into line with all the bug-eyed, buck-toothed rabbits, like a creature from an old B horror movie—*Attack of the Killer Rabbit*. I felt my stomach drop and my ears burn with embarrassment. Jim could only hold that look for so long before he dissolved into laughter.

Jim had a genius for working with people. Some might say that his techniques were sophisticated management methods, but when I reflect on his style, I keep coming back to one thing. Jim treated all of us like his friends, plain and simple, with respect and admiration.

Losing Jim was one of the most difficult challenges we all faced in our *Sesame Street* lives. Only two weeks before he died in 1990, he had asked me to appear with him on *The Arsenio Hall Show*. He was battling a little sore throat, but other than that he was feeling fine. I did a bit with my character Clifford and Jim was Kermit. We had a great time and the studio audience gave us a rousing thumbs-up with lots of laughter and applause. I didn't see Jim again after that.

His memorial service lasted for five hours, but it passed by as quickly as if it were one. I suppose I didn't want those moments to end because I wanted to go on celebrating Jim and his life forever. Caroll Spinney as Big Bird came out and sang Jim's signature song, "It's Not Easy Being Green," and we did our best to honor Jim's wish that the event be like the rest of his life—fun and festive. (Though his death was sudden, Jim had made it clear to his friends and family what he would want at his memorial service.) He asked that we all wear bright-colored clothes. As a tribute and to honor Jim's request, Steve Whitmire bought a white suit for the occasion. He and his wife dyed it Kermit Green and cut out a collar just like Kermit's that he wore around his neck as a tie.

As I sat there, I imagined that Jim was looking down on us, loving the sea of colors assembled—just like the rainbow connection of fur, feathers, and fabric he brought to life for us all.

Not surprisingly, going back to work after a long and emotional ten days of both mourning and celebrating his life wasn't easy. But we knew Jim wanted his legacy to continue. He was very much on our minds, and he remains a presence to this day. We all want to keep Jim laughing up there, and I hope he's enjoying what we've done.

I learned so much about my craft from Jim, but I also learned a lot about what it means to be a professional and how to conduct myself as an empathetic "boss." We work for a big company, and Jim was the head of a global enterprise, but he ran it like it was a small family operation. He praised us both openly and privately. We didn't have formal performance reviews with him; instead, every now and then he'd say, "What are you doing for dinner?"

Over the meal, he'd always ask about your family and talk about his, as well. He'd share his thoughts about the show and your performance, but it was conversational and not confrontational, as if he were a friend, not a boss. The last time he and I got together like that was when he was in negotiations with Disney to take control of his businesses. During this time he kept me and everyone else apprised of what was going on.

Jim wanted us to be comfortable and to assure us that he had all our interests at heart. That night he also told me how much he liked what I was doing with Elmo and that he had another character in mind for me. We never got around to discussing it; we both thought there would be time enough for that later on. We topped off the nice evening by driving by a local movie theater that was showing the *Teenage Mutant Ninja Turtle* movie, which had just opened that weekend. The Jim Henson Creature Shop, a separate company he maintained, had built all the characters, and I had performed in the film.

Jim took great delight in seeing how many kids were dressed in costumes as they waited in a line that wrapped around the building. "Congratulations, Kevin," he said, and somehow the way he spoke those simple words made me feel as though I were the one responsible for its success.

After Jim's passing, the Henson family shared a few letters and notes he had written to us (he had written these thoughts down well in advance of his illness—just another thing he wanted to do for the people around him), expressing his feelings and his appreciation for our work and rallying us to continue the tradition when he was gone. With that wish in mind, we filmed a tribute to Jim that was later televised. In one scene, all the Muppets are backstage talking when Steve Whitmire as Kermit discovers them there and asks, "What are you guys doing? We've got a show to do!" True enough.

I'm grateful that I had the opportunity to work with Jim. And I'm especially grateful that he treated me like a friend.

• • •

ELMO RELIES ON his friends for many things. Sometimes he goes to them for comfort, as he did when he couldn't sleep and he asked Oscar for a hug. (Even the legendary grouch had to give in—after checking both ways to be certain no one was watching and securing a promise from Elmo that he wouldn't tell anyone.) Sometimes he relies on them to be his teachers, as many children do. In one recent segment, Elmo learned the word "no" from a young Muppet bully in the street. I'm sure parents can identify with the power that one little word has in the lives of their children.

Elmo loved the sound of the word, but didn't really understand its meaning. The novelty of it appealed to him, and he was itching to use it. (This may sound like a three-year-old in your life.) Then Gordon and Miles came over and asked Elmo if he wanted to play miniature golf. They knew that Elmo loved to play, so they were really surprised when he said no to Gordon.

Gordon asked again.

"No!"

"Well, okay, Elmo. We're going to leave." And they did.

Elmo looked at the camera and sadly asked, "Why did Elmo do that?"

It was exciting to have a new word, but this one wasn't working for him. Elmo was using the word too much and in the wrong situations. It was keeping him from doing the things he loved to do, and he was growing uncharacteristically unhappy.

When Maria and Luis asked him what was wrong, Elmo told them about the bully who'd given him the word and how it was making him do things he didn't mean to do. They found the bully—he'd been giving other kids the wrong words, too, and like Elmo, they were worried and unhappy—and asked him to leave the street.

On one level, the show was about drugs, but it also demonstrated the importance of friendship in Elmo's life. He has people who know him well, who share his interests, who want to spend time with him doing the things he loves to do, and who also watch out for him and are protective of him. While kids may get the antidrug message only through a guided conversation with adults, the lessons about friendship are clear.

For *Sesame Street*'s thirty-fifth anniversary in 2004, we shot a special "Elmo's World" that shows Elmo at his best. Writers Lou Berger and Judy Freudberg put together a team to create *The Street We Live On*. I had a great time starring in it with Elmo and also directing with Ken Diego and Victor Di Napoli.

The video opens with Grover dressed as a mail carrier. He's given the assignment of delivering a package to Oscar the Grouch and sets off from the Mail It center. "I'm a monster with a mission," he says, making his way down the block. Sesame Street is teeming with activity, but Grover is not to be deterred; he sees everyone from Alan to Zoe but can't stop to chat. "I have no time to dilly-dally!" Nearly exhausted from the effort, he reaches Oscar's can.

It turns out the package is from Elmo. Inside is a picture he's made and a note from his mom, which Oscar reads out loud: " 'Elmo drew this picture of Dorothy and accidentally spilled some spaghetti dinner on it. I thought you would like it.' Like it, heh, I LOVE it. The kid's a genius. Look," Oscar says, admiring the glob of pasta and sauce on the drawing. "Mixed media! Where is the little red menace?"

From that point forward, it's a look at Sesame Street from Elmo's point of view, as the action shifts to the set of "Elmo's World" and he meets and interacts with the residents on Sesame Street.

Elmo considers them all friends, and he even laughs when Oscar tells him to get lost. ("Elmo loves Oscar!" he says. "Oh, yuck," groans the grouch.) Elmo is his usual upbeat self, but there's an extra spring in his step and gleam in his eye, since he's been thinking about Sesame Street and finding ways to welcome every one of his friends into his world. Dorothy has a Sesame Street sign in her bowl. His TV is tuned to the Grover, Maria, Big Bird, and All Elmo's Friends Channel. Mr. Noodle shows the audience how to eat a cookie like Cookie Monster. Super Grover takes Elmo on a sweet and funny journey through the past, "to the Sesame Street that was!" And finally Elmo returns to his world, still thinking of his friends. Some, like Bert and Ernie, he doesn't see as often as others, like Zoe and Telly. That doesn't matter; whether they live just around the corner or miles and miles away, whether they are monsters or grouches, birds or bears, they're all his friends. All he has to do is think of them, and they're right there beside him.

And that's the way I feel about friends—you can always pick up just where you left off, whether you see each other every day or twice a year, whether you have a million pals or a handful of close companions, whether you know them from childhood or work or the corner grocery.

Maybe you can't be together as much as you'd like, but there are so many ways to stay in touch. Even the simplest gestures—doing a small favor, making a quick phone call, sending a note or a photo or even a spaghetti-stained package—can bring joy and make you feel connected. Like Elmo, you can keep your friends close, just by thinking of them.

7

COOPERATION

IN MY FAMILY, we defined "cooperation" as "four children sleeping in a single bedroom." I've heard friends and colleagues fussing about having had to share a room with another sibling, but try tripling that. And let's just remember that our last name was Clash.

Nevertheless, we managed to find space for Ne-Ne's interest in modern dance, Georgie's sports fanaticism, my puppetry, and Pam's increasing Barbie collection, all shoehorned into a space we somehow divided up and enjoyed.

Maybe in exchange for having to share a room, our parents gave us a free hand when it came to decorating our domain. We were children of the 1970s, so we painted the walls with fluorescent paint—pink, lime green, yellow. Ne-Ne loved black-light posters, and in addition to staring at glow-in-the-dark stars stuck to the ceiling, we drifted off to the nuclear glow of "Love Power!" and R. Crumb's "Keep on Trucking" as well as images of bands like the Jackson Five. The black-light glow and neon colors made me feel like I was living in a lava lamp.

We each carved out our own niche in the room. I had some puppets and supplies there, but the overflow of my creations spilled onto the yellow shelves in my parents' bedroom. George favored football and basketball posters; Dr. J floated in that spectral light always about to jam the ball through the hoop. Ne-Ne was into anything cool and groovy. Pam was still a little girl, with a collection of dolls and stuffed animals, all of them wearing wide-eyed, dazed expressions, as if they were reacting to our decor.

WE MANAGED TO make it work—most of the time. When Ne-Ne got older and started socializing more, I wasn't allowed in the room when she was hanging with her girlfriends. I didn't like playing the pesky little brother role, and I hated being away from my puppet-making supplies, but my mother insisted I give her the space she needed.

Feeling dejected, I would leave the house, head for the construction site of the Francis Scott Key Bridge, and sit on the recently poured roadway waiting for someone to discover I had run away from home. I imagined my family arriving to beg forgiveness, to tell me how wrong they'd been to kick me out of my space, to soothe me with offerings of lasagna—my favorite.

I'd sit on that bridge watching my house for any signs of them heading out to find me. I'd wait, and I'd wait, and I'd wait some more. Then my growling stomach would betray me, and I'd remember that I'd already missed the *ABC After-School Special* and I was about to miss *The Beverly Hillbillies*. And so I'd trudge home, defeated by my weak will but cheered by the thoughts of dinnertime and the small screen. Hadn't anyone noticed that I'd been gone?

Sometimes, on my way home, I'd stop off to visit our neighbor Miss Marie DeLoach, an elderly woman with no teeth. She reminded me of the black comic Moms Mabley, whom I'd seen on *The Mike Douglas Show*. Miss Marie didn't have Moms's sharp wit, but she offered me something else—her respect and admiration. Miss Marie loved my puppets and, by extension, me. "Kevin," she'd say, "you just keep at it. You're going to do something big with those puppets one of these days."

MISS MARIE KNEW of my growing reputation as the neighborhood Ed Sullivan, since I'd been doing backyard shows for the local kids starting at the age of nine. The first show I ever did was adapted from a story I found in a frayed, coverless children's book we had at home. The details are now hazy, but it involved a dog puppet and a sailboat—both of which I built myself.

These early public performances were a cooperative effort. To entice my audience, I offered free treats I bought from a neighbor, Miss Fleming, who ran a candy store out of her home. My mother helped

153

hang the bedsheet I used as a stage (I'd poke my puppets over the top and stay hidden behind it), and I even enlisted the aid of Orlando to serve as chief "shusher"—he'd spirit away any of the kids who cried uncontrollably and distracted the others.

Eventually everyone in my family and quite a few people in the neighborhood and at school helped me out. A classmate's mom donated the ballet tutus her daughter outgrew for my "costume shop"; sometimes I would be given foam, fabric, or other supplies for puppet and set building; Lee McCullough, my friend Lorraine's mother, was a constant source of encouragement and made the second-best biscuits on earth. (No one can ever outbake a boy's grandmother.) At various times, different neighbors and friends lent my father their vans or trucks when my productions grew too elaborate to fit in the Get Out and Push.

Once I began putting on shows locally, my father was instrumental in helping me find a larger audience and grow as a performer and artist. He was not only my driver, chauffeuring me and a carload of puppets and equipment from one gig to another; he also helped me build the sets and stages. Besides teaching me to sew and helping me with my earliest efforts, my mother served as my PR department by helping to get the word out about a show, and was my head of marketing and educational research, letting me know when an audience got restless or when they really enjoyed a particular bit. She didn't go to my shows just to watch me—she was watching the crowd's reaction, too! Mom showed her belief in me by doing things like tracking down Kermit Love or reaching out to local people who she thought would be of help to me. Whether it was at a local church, a downtown Baltimore department store, a waterfront festival, or later, a local television studio, my parents were ever-present and uncomplaining.

When I finally got my break in local television, it was due to the generosity and encouragement of Stu Kerr, my first mentor. Stu was a television fixture in Baltimore on the local CBS affiliate WMAR, where he was more than the news announcer and weatherman, though that was how he started his career there.

Stu had a flair for improv and comedy, and was a popular children's entertainer because of his weekend children's variety show— *Professor Kool's Fun School*—which featured games, activities, and live entertainment. (He also had been our local "Bozo the Clown" on that syndicated program, and was always developing characters that young viewers would respond to.) Before I met Kermit Love, before I met Jim Henson, I met Stu Kerr.

When I was fifteen, I performed at the annual Heritage Fair in Dundalk, where Stu was also doing a show. During a break, he came to see me do my thing, though I didn't know he was in the audience. I had brought along several puppets, including my mother-and-daughter skunks who belted out Helen Reddy's "You and Me Against the World." I also did spoofs of popular commercials from the 1970s. My mummy puppet sang the old Band-Aid's song, "I am stuck on Band-Aids brand, 'cause Band-Aid's stuck on me . . ."; my hamburger puppet had fun with the famous McDonald's jingle, "Two all-beef patties, special sauce, lettuce, cheese, pickles, onions on a sesame seed bun."

After I was done, he approached my parents and me and explained that he was auditioning performers for a new show. "I'm impressed with what I just saw, Kevin," he said. "I think you'd be good for what we have in mind."

Because of my age, I had to have my parents' approval, but they readily agreed to let me try out. This was a big deal, my first break into a regular gig on local television. Up to now, I'd had bits and pieces of my shows broadcast on the local news; "the kid with the puppets" often made for good copy in the local papers, as well. Under Stu's tutelage, I honed my puppetry skills and was soon performing with him on the new show he created, wrote, and starred in, *Caboose*, where I would work off and on as I finished up high school. We would shoot every Friday after school, and Stu went out of his way to work around my schedule.

Stu was a wonderful man with a marvelous sense of humor, and he was the perfect teacher for me. Before working with Stu, I had never used a script. I simply had an outline in my head for what I was planning to do in any given show, a fine improvisational style since I was working alone. Television, however, was another matter entirely. Stu taught me about comic timing and how to interpret a writer's words. He also taught me a lot about the business, which involved the cooperative efforts of many.

As an amateur, I had to work with lots of people behind the scenes to get my shows off the ground, but I still was more of a solo artist. I was not used to working with writers, directors, producers, and other performers. I'd never had a boss before. I had to learn the elaborate dance of give-and-take that all performing artists must do in order to succeed. Stu had the perfect combination of patience and experience to help me gain a firm foothold in the medium of television and in the grown-up world of work.

Stu had been in the military with Bob Keeshan of *Captain Kangaroo* fame, and they later worked together at NBC as pages. When it came time for this fledgling to fly, Stu not only nudged me out of the nest, he found a safe place for me to land—on one of the best-known children's shows in the history of television. Through Stu's efforts, Bob Keeshan saw a few of the *Caboose* shows I'd done and he liked my work—enough to hire me. I was still very young, but because of Stu, I was working on *Captain Kangaroo*.

Captain Kangaroo was, of course, a national show, and that meant jumping out of the small pond and diving into a very big, very deep one, which happened to be based in New York. By the time I began performing on the show, *Captain Kangaroo* had long been considered a children's classic, its host an icon. I had been hired to be an assistant puppeteer and builder, initially part time, which meant that I commuted back and forth between Baltimore and New York, staying in a Holiday Inn on Manhattan's West Side, near the CBS studios on West Fifty-seventh Street where the show was taped. I guess it was a tough schedule, but I was young and I never gave it a second thought because I was so happy to be performing.

The *Captain Kangaroo* producers even came down to Turner's Station, right into my house and into my parents' bedroom, where they went to the yellow shelves and picked a few of my own characters who would appear on the show. They especially liked a dog called Francine Fuzzy, a silver-haired kid named Artie, and an anteater creature with a snout only a mother could love. The puppets I'd made at my kitchen table, with their Jo-Ann Fabrics fur and fleece, were going to be on national television, with their own story lines and supporting characters!

By the time I graduated from Dundalk High in 1979, I was doing regular guest spots on *Captain Kangaroo* and hoping to get on *Sesame Street*. Things were happening so quickly that I never considered stopping my work to go on to college, and my parents certainly didn't press that issue. I had a shot at making my passion into my career, and they were behind me all the way. (Funny enough, I sometimes appeared as "Kevin the College Student" on *Captain Kangaroo*.)

I almost had the rug pulled out from under me, though, that summer after graduation. While all my classmates were making plans—college, the army, a job, a move—I was convinced that *Sesame Street* was going to come calling. The local papers even ran a story on how I was headed for show biz, that soon I'd be hanging with the likes of Big Bird and Ernie.

Thanks to Kermit Love, I had been able to get into the *Sesame*

Street studios when I was in New York, where I would absorb what I could. I just knew that someone would notice me and give me my big break. I had actually auditioned for Jim Henson after I did the Macy's parade, but Kermit had reminded Jim I had a commitment to *Caboose* so that hadn't gone anywhere.

Now, after graduating, I had about as much common sense as one of my puppets when I boldly turned down a full-time job with *Captain Kangaroo* and quit *Caboose*, convinced that there was a job (and a rent-controlled brownstone apartment) waiting for me on *Sesame Street*. But they weren't knocking down my door with an offer. Meanwhile, *Caboose* hired someone else to take my place—a gifted ventriloquist named Todd Stockman—and that train, so to speak, left the station without me. I'd said no to the Captain. So now I had no stage and no audience. Fate wasn't cooperating with me.

Miraculously, the Captain came calling once more at the end of that summer, the job offer still in hand. This time I said yes, and I made the move to New York for good. Because I was full time, I no longer got free lodging courtesy of the show at the Holiday Inn. Since it was convenient for me to be near the CBS studios where we taped, I found a room at the George Washington Hotel, a cheap residential hotel on the Upper West Side of Manhattan. They must have offered a honeymoon suite (or an hourly rate) because nearly every night as I tried to get comfortable on the sagging excuse for a mattress, I was treated to the sounds of amorous athletics taking place on the opposite side of the wall, just inches from my head.

Finally, I had arrived in New York to stay. True, my cramped bunk on New Pittsburgh Avenue was heaven compared to this sorry lump of a bed, and I could have used some earplugs, but I was where I wanted to be, doing what I loved.

I WAS HAVING a blast on *Captain Kangaroo*, puppeteering and building puppets. (I also did some acting, but I was always more comfortable in front of the camera when I had a puppet on my arm.) Whenever I could, I continued to haunt the *Sesame Street* studios, making connections, learning how the show was put together, and, of course, filling in whenever and however I could.

The first time I walked out onto that set, my pulse shot up. *You mean, that's the stoop? That's really Mr. Hooper's store?* Even in the harsh glare of the work lights, the set seemed so real to me, I could almost smell the rice and beans coming from the second-story window of the brownstone and hear the laughter of children as they clattered down the front steps and onto the sidewalks to jump rope and play hopscotch. I could just picture Big Bird coming through those doors and saying "Hi, welcome to Sesame Street!" I was in awe when I got my picture taken with Big Bird, and I felt like a kid again.

After about six months of living in New York full time, on Kermit Love's recommendation, I auditioned for and got a second job on a show he was involved in, *The Great Space Coaster*. The show was an internationally syndicated half-hour children's program combining live action, music, and puppets (I played Goriddle Gorilla, among others) that Kermit had designed and built. I was having a great time, even though I was holding down two full-time jobs, plus working a little at *Sesame Street* and building puppets for the Captain in the evening.

The authentic—too authentic—New York atmosphere of the George Washington Hotel, however, finally lost its appeal (as did the lack of kitchen facilities—steam table take-out was a stomach-churning risk I was tired of taking). With so much work, I could finally afford to leave George and my loud nocturnal neighbors behind and get an apartment. I eventually found a place with another *Coaster* cast member, Jim Martin. Like me, Jim would go on to work at *Sesame Street*, where he is still a puppeteer and director. After living in various sublets in the Village and elsewhere, we landed in Hell's Kitchen, on Forty-seventh Street and Tenth Avenue.

My shared bedroom and work space back home proved to be a great test run for cooperation, because Jim and I were splitting an apartment that was tiny, even by Manhattan standards. The very small main area served as kitchen, living room, dining room, and puppet-building workshop.

The quarters were cramped, but Jim and I were working on the same projects and were only there late at night. My schedule was this: From six in the morning until one o'clock in the afternoon, I was at the *Captain Kangaroo* studios shooting. From two in the afternoon until six at night, I was performing on *The Great Space Coaster*. From six-thirty to midnight, I was in a recording studio for that show. At midnight I headed home, where Jim and I went to work building puppets for the Captain.

Jim was a great help with my construction assignments, and as much of a workaholic as me. We had so little space (he was a true pack rat, like my dad, which made our apartment really feel like home to me), and I had so little time that we worked in shifts. He'd take the first two hours at the table, and I'd take the next two or however many necessary to get the job done. Then we'd crash until it was time to get up and head for the studio. Getting a full eight hours of sleep in those days wasn't a priority (or a possibility).

An experienced builder, Jim knew exactly where we could find the right materials for the puppets. Jo-Ann Fabrics had served me well, but New York's fabric district offered a mind-boggling selection of choices. We had generous network budgets for purchasing puppet-building materials, and Jim eliminated a lot of my confusion by steering me to the right suppliers every time. Jim became a close friend, and when my daughter was born I asked him to be her godfather.

Interestingly, though the quality (and expense) of the materials I was using was much higher, the puppets we made and that I saw on the sets of all the shows still worked and moved in the same simple fashion that puppeteers had been practicing forever. Yes, this was the big time, but the simple, classic puppetry skills I'd learned as a youngster and refined as I grew older were proving to be a perfect foundation for my work on *Captain* and *Coaster*. Similarly, all of my local television experience had prepared me well for what I was doing now and for what was to come.

AFTER ABOUT THREE years or so, I was officially offered the chance to do ten shows with *Sesame Street* for the 1983 season. It seemed that my unofficial temping and interning had finally paid off, and I couldn't wait to sign the contract.

It was standard practice that shows like *Sesame Street* would work around the featured performers' and puppeteers' schedules when they could—but not for part-time players like me, as they usually worked more than one gig. Since I was busy with *Captain* and *Coaster*, I called the person who handled the scheduling to explain my situation. *Sesame Street* did more than a hundred shows, so I figured it would be easy to find ten that fit my schedule. I was stunned when I was told that under no circumstances could they work with my schedule. They didn't want to talk to Ron Kreidman, the lawyer I'd hired to do the negotiations (who is my lawyer still). Why couldn't they cooperate with me on this? I was willing to be flexible. They weren't.

I wanted to work with *Sesame Street* and Jim Henson very badly, and I didn't want to start off on a sour note, so I agreed to let them tear up my contract. Hard as it was, I figured it was best to just walk away and not create any ill will.

I continued my work on *Captain* and *Coaster* for a few more years, keeping in touch with my *Sesame Street* connections. One day I got a call from Jim's wife, Jane Henson, who was involved in recruiting new talent for Jim's various ventures. She asked me if I wanted to help with some puppeteering workshops she was leading for the Jim Henson Company. I'd be involved in training new puppeteers for the Henson organization. I eagerly accepted. My strategy worked, and I was on my way to Sesame Street!

Stu Kerr's lessons on cooperation—learning to work with other professionals in areas ranging from the creative and artistic to the business and financial side—really were paying off. But every once in a while, my youthful ambition would get ahold of me and I'd need a refresher course. Kermit Love often stepped in to do the job.

While I was still on *Captain* and *Coaster*, I got a call from one of the producers of an upcoming Jim Henson film, *The Dark Crystal*. Duncan Kenworthy, who would go on to produce many hits, including *Four Weddings and a Funeral*, wanted to know if I might be interested in talking further about performing in the movie, as it would involve lots of special puppeteering effects. I was psyched—I would be working with Jim *and* doing a movie. Even better, I would get to spend eight months living and working in London at Jim's Creature Shop.

I called Kermit to tell him about the opportunity, as I was sure an offer was pending. I was so excited I was talking a hundred miles an hour, and when I paused for a breath, I heard Kermit's patient sigh. The man had become like a grandfather to me, as he had for a whole generation of designers and puppeteers, and I'd come to recognize that sound.

"So you see a problem with me doing this, then?"

"Kevin, keep in mind two things. One, you've made a commitment to two shows. You should honor that commitment. You don't want to be known in the business as someone who puts his interests ahead of the show. Two, you've got work on two series. Series work is steady work. Let's say you go to London, do the film. You come back to nothing. Security is a good thing. Stick with it. They'll ask you again."

Though I hated saying no to Jim, I knew deep down that Kermit was right. On his recommendation, I went through with the meeting and even got an offer, but I had to tell Jim himself that I was declining.

Turning down that offer was one of the hardest things I had to do, but it was the right thing. With Kermit's support, I was gaining the confidence I needed to take control of my career and my future. And I was reminded, once again, that this is a business that's based on group efforts and on being cooperative.

FROM THE VERY beginning, *Sesame Street* was designed to be a model neighborhood in which people and creatures of all colors, shapes, and sizes could work together to resolve problems and live in harmony. Whether the day's events revolve around something serious, such as Gordon and Susan's adoption of Miles, or something fun, like Alan's plan to host a karaoke night at Mr. Hooper's, you'll always find the characters willing to cooperate to achieve a common goal.

After Alan announces his idea, everyone gets very excited about being able to sing along with the karaoke machine. Elmo is especially excited because it's a nighttime event. "Boy," he says with a laugh, "Elmo gets to stay up late and sing with everybody on Sesame Street!"

Adults and Muppets sign up to sing, and no one fights over who will be first or next—this is a very cooperative bunch, after all. Everyone is eager to share their talent and love of singing, but Telly is nervous as he waits for his turn onstage. His good buddy Baby Bear (played by David Rudman) continues to encourage him between the others' songs. "I'll sing before you and then you can see how easy it is," he promises Telly (played by Marty Robinson). "There's nothing to it."

"Buh-Bay-Bay-Baby Bear, I-I-I'm not so sure about this."

"Telly, if I can do it, you can do it, believe me."

But Baby Bear's enthusiasm gets the better of him, and he freezes up in front of the microphone, with all those people and Muppets watching him. Now, I did a lot of talent shows and variety shows in high school, and the typical audience there would not have responded the way the *Sesame Street* audience does. Everyone offers encouragement to Baby Bear, but it's his friend Telly who comes to his aid.

"Oh no, Baby Bear's in trouble! Don't worry, Baby Bear, I'll help you!" he calls out, rushing onto the stage. Once there, he forgets his own fear as he looks out into the audience and tells Baby Bear, "Everybody out there is your friend. They all just wanna hear ya sing. Come on, come on, I'll do it with ya. Hit it, Alan."

After they successfully deliver their song—as a duet—Baby Bear says, "Thank you, thank you, I did it!"

"I did it, too!" says Telly.

"*We* did it!" they cheer together, and the lesson is clear.

Because this is *Sesame Street*, though, the lesson is strengthened a few moments later when the karaoke machine goes on the fritz. It looks as if the evening will be cut short and those who didn't get their turn will be disappointed.

"Sorry, everybody," says Alan. "I think the machine is broken . . . what can I say, it's a rental."

Of course, the residents of *Sesame Street* come through in a spontaneous display of cooperation. Telly offers to get his tuba, Rosita her guitar, Zoe her tambourine, Gladys her harmonica, and Elmo his drum. Who needs a machine when you have a talented group of musicians who can accompany the singers? Who needs the spotlight when the entire cast has more fun together, singing "We Are the People in Our Neighborhood"?

With Elmo playing his drum and pigs and cows and monsters and birds all joining in, we're reminded again of that joyful noise that music can be, and the even more joyful noise of people working together, sharing experiences, and making lasting memories as a group.

Working through the karaoke catastrophe was a wonderful example of a previous lesson taking root and bearing fruit. In an episode from an earlier season, UN Secretary-General Kofi Annan once had to resolve a dispute among the Muppets regarding who got to sing the alphabet. "There is no problem," he tells them. "You simply need to cooperate. You can all sing the alphabet song together." Afterward, the Muppets jostle each other to be first in line to congratulate Mr. Annan on this latest conflict resolution, but Telly says, "I know, let's do this the United Nations way!" "Yeah, group hug!" cries Elmo, and Kofi Annan and Muppets all hug and congratulate each other at the same time.

IT TOOK A truly collaborative effort for Elmo to reach the level of recognition and popularity that he enjoys, and the same kind of co-operation was necessary to bring out the wildly popular Tickle Me Elmo doll in 1996.

Two inventors came to the new product buyers at Tyco Preschool with an idea. After seeing two laughing children tickling each other in the park, Ron Druben imagined a toy that would giggle when tick-led. His friend Greg Hyman designed the circuitry enabling Tickles the Monkey to laugh when it was touched in specific places. Each time the monkey was touched, he laughed a little more.

Stan Clutton, the head of marketing and of research and develop-ment, reviewed the product and passed on it; that arm of Tyco Preschool did only plastic, not plush, toys at the time. But he was im-pressed enough to send the monkey to a colleague who oversaw a line of Looney Tunes toys at another division of Tyco. The idea behind Tickles the Monkey was strong, but the Tyco folks felt that the toy needed more personality. For a while, they tossed around the idea of creating a Tickle Taz toy, based on the Warner Bros. cartoon character the Tasmanian Devil.

While that idea was under consideration, Tyco Preschool gained the rights to *Sesame Street* toys, including plush ones. Elmo's signature laugh was the perfect voice for the toy. Stan Clutton immediately phoned his colleague and asked him to send back the laugh mechanism—they were going to use it in an Elmo doll.

Tyco sent a prototype to the advertising agency. Advertising is a visual medium, and for television ads, the executives felt that the toy was too static. It didn't really *do* anything. Back went the Laughing Elmo prototype to the design group headed by Amanda van Holt. A vibrating mechanism had been in use for a while, but no one had paired it with a plush toy that laughed when touched. The combination of the sound chip containing me laughing as Elmo and the vibrating mechanism produced Tickle Me Elmo. Neil Friedman, head of Tyco Preschool at the time, planned to roll it out as its number-one toy for the holiday season.

The toy was so popular that Cartier Jewelers put a million-dollar Tiffany necklace around a Tickle Me Elmo doll—buy the necklace get the doll. Rosie O'Donnell took a liking to the little guy, gave away hundreds of them on her talk show, and fed the mania. We've all heard the stories about desperate and fighting parents. As I mentioned, Whoopi Goldberg has been an ardent supporter of *Sesame Street* for a long time. Shortly after the holiday craze of '96, she and I were both on Rosie's show, along with Luther Vandross.

During a commercial break she turned to me and said, "Let me tell you what I went through with these damn Tickle Me Elmos!"

Whoopi put on her trademark glare but had a teasing glint in her eye as she stared me down over her glasses. "Well, thanks to you, I went to get a couple of those dolls for my grandkids, and some woman pulled a couple of my dreads out trying to get ahead of me. I oughta send you the bill for getting them fixed!"

I WAS HELPED by many people along the way, in so many different ways. But over and over again, they all taught me a similar lesson: Cooperation means more than simply being in agreement with another person. It means offering encouragement and aid, working together to resolve conflicts, compromising and sharing. From tiny backyard shows with a sheet pinned to a clothesline as a stage, to television productions and multimillion-dollar movies involving countless collaborators, to a doll that inspired irrational behavior and hair-yanking, my life as a performer has never been a solo act.

No life ever is.

8

LEARNING

O**KAY, CLASS," SAID** our social studies teacher, drawing our flagging attention to the front of the classroom. "Let's get started." I glanced at the clock and tried not to fidget. Twelve-twenty; only about two and a half hours of school left to go. Would this dreary January day never end?

I wasn't a bad student in junior high, but my grades weren't the best in the class, and I didn't particularly love to read like some of the other kids, who couldn't get enough of *The Hardy Boys* or *Nancy Drew*. Put a copy of the latest *TV Guide* in my hands, though, and I could easily get engrossed. But needless to say, that was not on our teacher's recommended reading list. Now she held up our textbook, *Many Peoples, Many Places*, and announced something that made me stifle a groan.

"It's oral report time! This project will count for one-half of your grade on this unit."

Ugh.

"I'm going to assign each of you a partner to work with and a country to report on," she continued, pulling the globe from a bookshelf and carrying it to her desk. "And I'm going to do this completely at random, just to be fair."

She gave the globe a spin before explaining that we'd be drawing numbers from a hat to pick our partners and playing a version of pin the tail on the donkey to choose our country. But instead of a donkey, we used the enormous world map that hung on one wall. She'd devised a system involving more numbered slips of paper, and somehow it was all supposed to work out evenly.

Within minutes, I learned that my partner was a guy named Armand. He wasn't an extraordinary student, but a nice reliable friend who was good at reading aloud—an activity that made my blood run cold and my cheeks burn hot with embarrassment. Despite my growing comfort level in front of an audience, reading in front of my classmates was a far cry from performing with my puppets.

Armand and I ended up with Russia—as in the entire, enormous Soviet Union, since this was well before it broke into separate countries. I was terrified at the thought of having to get up in front of the class and report on the Soviet economy, agriculture, natural resources, transportation systems, weather, and customs. What did I know about Russia? That it got really cold there? That they always won a lot of gold medals at the Olympics? Where would we begin?

"One-half of your grade will be based on the factual content. One-half will be based on the creativity of your presentation. That means that I expect to see visual aids—charts, graphs, photos, and the like," my teacher announced.

I started to relax. That was cool. I could draw. Armand could do the talking, and I could design and make the visual aids. And somehow, we'd find a way to divide up the research. A moment later that idea was squashed.

"I also expect that each partner will speak the same amount."

I spent the rest of the day with my stomach in knots—even though the project wasn't due for anther two weeks. Armand and I agreed to talk in study hall the next day. That night as I lay in bed staring at the glow-in-dark stars on our ceiling, I came up with a fabulous idea.

On presentation day, while the rest of the kids in the class lugged poster boards, plaster-of-Paris relief maps, and assorted other objects, Armand and I carried a suitcase holding a puppet and costumes that I'd made especially for the project and a compact portfolio of visual aids.

Inspired by how much I enjoyed watching Kermit the Frog as a reporter, I got Armand to dress like a TV journalist, complete with a trench coat, a microphone, and a fedora with a "PRESS" card stuck in the brim. Armand would assume the role of interviewer and ask my Russian expert puppets questions about their homeland. I had a single puppet but two sets of costumes—for a man and a woman—so I made them into a husband-and-wife duo. I sat nervously through a few presentations before we volunteered to go next.

Armand was a great interviewer, and with a puppet on my hand, it was easy for me to talk in front of the class. I thought it went pretty well, but I was concentrating so hard on just getting all the facts out, I couldn't be sure. After we finished, we got much more than the usual polite applause that our teacher required of each audience. I settled back in my seat, pleased with their laughter and relieved it was all over.

When the bell rang, I gathered up my books and folders and tucked my puppet back into my suitcase, standing up to merge with the rest of the kids filing out of the classroom. I felt a tap on my shoulder, and my teacher asked me to wait for a moment. Armand was already standing at her desk, shuffling his feet and gently clapping one of the erasers on the board, creating a small cloud of chalk dust.

"Armand, Kevin, I just wanted to tell you how very much I enjoyed your presentation. You really held everyone's attention. It was excellent."

We would find out just how excellent she thought it was when we were told that we'd been selected to present the report to an all-school assembly along with students who'd done the best reports in other classes. A few weeks later, Armand and I stood in front of the entire student body to do our presentation for a second time. But I didn't view it as simply repeating our report in front of more students. It was an encore performance, in front of an audience who reacted with genuine laughter and applause. Even though I was still young, I could tell that their response was the real thing. As a result of this presentation, I got my first real media coverage. I was written up in the local paper (the now-defunct *News-American*) and made the cover of their insert magazine, *Young World*.

That experience had a profoundly positive impact on me. I enjoyed school, but I was hardly a stand-out student. Early on, I'd never been that interested in reading and struggled with it. For me to do the research on a project was never easy, mostly because I lacked the desire to learn about a place like Russia. What did that have to do with me in Turner's Station? Adding the creative element to the assignment sparked my interest and got me excited about what I had to do. From then on, I tried to find a way to incorporate my interests into my schoolwork. Similarly, I got interested in reading because it was a way to learn about one of my favorite subjects—television. You already know that I treated *TV Guide* like a favorite comic book, but I also was drawn to magazines like *People*, where I would pore over longer articles and profiles of my favorite stars. It wasn't Shakespeare, but it got me reading.

That a reluctant reader and sometimes unmotivated learner wound up making a career of teaching children through a landmark educational television program isn't ironic; it's absolutely fitting and right.

• • •

WHEN WE TAKE the time to be creative in our teaching, chances are that we'll be more successful in engaging a child's mind. On *Sesame Street* and "Elmo's World," we strive to make that effort, with specific educational goals in mind. But before the writers ever put pen to paper or a Muppeteer gives life to a character, many decisions must be made about the direction a particular season, episode, or scene will take. Everything begins with the curriculum.

Dr. Rosemarie Truglio, who is in charge of research and education for the show, heads a staff of professional educators who establish a set of curriculum goals for a season. For example, they decided for the 2005 season, our thirty-sixth, to focus on health. The educational staff consulted with experts on nutritional, physical, and mental health needs of children. (Perhaps you saw the "exercise moment" with Elmo on PBS, where he urges young viewers to get up and "move your body"—that's part of this initiative.) Once Rosemarie and her team completed their initial research, they convened a meeting of the show's writers, headed by Lou Berger, and producers, led by executive producer Carol-Lynn Parente, to explore how best to execute their goals.

The first step this group takes is a general discussion of what preschoolers today are like. After all, kids have changed over the years, and *Sesame Street* is constantly evolving to meet their changing needs and interests. Once the curriculum goals are established for the season, they are broken down into lessons that can be introduced show by show and then scene by scene.

As performers and writers, our first instincts are to go with what we believe will be the most entertaining way to get a message across. Once the scripts are developed, Rosemarie and her staff review them and suggest changes to make sure that the curricular objectives are clearly and explicitly expressed, that the show is age appropriate and safe. We know kids imitate what they see on television, and we want to be certain that nothing our characters do would ever put a child imitating them in any kind of jeopardy.

Once the theme is in place, we work age-appropriate school-readiness skills into the show. Reading fundamentals are always a primary consideration—letter recognition and letter sound. Along with verbal literacy, we emphasize numerical literacy (sometimes called numeracy) so that kids will be ready for school with the ABCs and their 123s mastered. Basic (and now classic) elements of the show—such as the letter of the day and the Count's number of the day—are all designed to reinforce these skills.

Sesame Street wouldn't be *Sesame Street* if we concentrated only on "school" learning. Any parent or teacher will tell you that social skills and emotional intelligence are equally important components of a child's education, so we work hard to deliver positive messages in those areas, as well. As a father, I know that the tried and true lessons of sharing and getting along well with others ("playing nice," as many of us parents simply say) are critical in a child's development.

Because virtually everything you see on *Sesame Street* and on "Elmo's World" is carefully orchestrated to teach, it's often difficult to isolate a single "message" within many of the scenes, since so many things are going on at once. One series of overlapping lessons involved Big Bird and his seagull pen pal Gulliver, who comes to Sesame Street for a visit. Big Bird can't wait to introduce Gulliver to all his wonderful friends, including monsters like Rosita and Baby Bear, humans like Gordon and Maria, and the full range of diverse residents who live on the street.

But Gulliver is puzzled. Looking at Rosita and Baby Bear, he says, "They're not birds! Are they your *friends*?" When Big Bird wants to play basketball with Gabi and Miles, Gulliver won't join in. "People?!!" he exclaims. "I like playing at home . . . on my bird team." Gulliver is used to hanging around with birds only, and the variety of monsters and humans is making him uncomfortable. When Big Bird announces that Gulliver is about to meet his best pal in the world, the gull is certain that he's going to be introduced to a fellow feathered friend.

And that's when Gulliver meets Snuffy—and shows his true colors.

"Snuffy isn't a bird!" he says, shocked.

"Uh, no, not today," Snuffy chuckles.

"Bu-bu-but he's your best friend . . . he's not a bird and I don't want to play with him. In my neighborhood birds only play with birds."

Big Bird is appalled at Gulliver's reaction and then stands up to him. "Listen, Gulliver, if you don't want to play with my best friend, then I don't want to play with you!"

The lessons of tolerance and inclusion are subtly conveyed. If you won't play nice with others, if you're not going to treat them with respect, if you can't be open to diversity, then you're not welcome in my world. Eventually Big Bird, Snuffy, and Gulliver do make their peace, and Gulliver learns to make friends with all the nonbirds who live on Sesame Street. "Wow, wait till I tell all the birds back home about this!" he exclaims.

FROM THE BEGINNING, "Elmo's World" was designed to immerse viewers in the imaginative mind of a fun-loving and hyperinquisitive three-and-a-half-year-old little monster. Other than the children who join him in the Mr. Noodle segments, Elmo is the only regular character on the show who speaks. He is our guide in his world, and that sends an empowering message to children and is a valuable lesson for parents.

It's often tempting to be the source of all information for our kids. They ask so many questions, and we have to resist the urge to just answer them all. The show is designed to demonstrate to kids that knowledge is power. I personally love the Mr. Noodle segments not only because of the physical comedy of Bill Irwin, but because it's the kids who are offering encouragement and instruction to an adult.

Elmo and all kids take great pleasure in being as smart as an adult. You've probably witnessed the abundant joy kids take in saying "Nooooooo!" to you when you give them a silly and obviously wrong bit of information. Kids love to feel in control and smart, and so does

Elmo. It's "Elmo's World" because, well . . . it *is* Elmo's world, and he's in charge of his own learning and discovering. Because he has the freedom to explore and define his own mission, he's an energized and enthusiastic student of the world.

From participating in "Elmo's World," I've learned that, as parents, we can sometimes set the agenda for our kids' learning, but we can't structure it so tightly that it becomes a means to an end, a search for a particular fact or answer, and nothing else. Elmo exhibits a child's natural curiosity and intelligence. While a subtle hand guides him in the initial direction he should go, his path may meander, he may go off track, but he's learning and having fun as he goes about his journey. That's the way it is for most kids.

I admire Elmo's persistence, as well. Each time he learns one thing about a subject, he's eager to pursue his quest further. Elmo always wants to know more. How many of us can say the same of our adult lives and our work? How many of us give up when the answers don't come easily?

In one scene, Elmo wants to go to the zoo. His insatiable curiosity has him itching in his fur. He approaches Maria to take him, but she's too busy. Elmo's disappointment registers in his whole body—but only for a few moments. Instead of spending the rest of the day sulking, he figures that if he can't go to the zoo, he will get the zoo to come to him. He rebounds and gets all of his friends to pretend to be zoo animals, and they teach him what he's so eager to know. Not only that, but because Maria is busy and said she wished she could take him, he brings his pretend zoo to her so she can share in his excitement. He solves the problem and enriches his own life and the lives of others. His uniquely creative solution to a problem models healthy, independent thinking for children.

Elmo is never afraid to ask questions or to admit that he doesn't know something, and over the years, I've realized that that's actually a smart way to behave. My formal education ended after high school, and then I moved to a city and began working in a field surrounded by many highly educated individuals, not to mention professionals who had lifetimes of experience compared to me. But I learned quickly not to let the potential for embarrassment prevent me from admitting I didn't know how to do something or have an answer.

Had I been reluctant to ask questions, I would never have risen from the ranks of puppeteer, to directing some of the shows, to becoming one of the producers. As a producer, I can offer input on projects from the get-go, in areas ranging from scripts, to props, to shots. I also head the puppeteering team and recruit new puppeteers. When I train them, I always find that the ones who are on the floor watching and asking questions even when they aren't in a scene are the ones who take their work to the next level more quickly.

Elmo's curiosity is a reflection of my personality, as well. When I first got the opportunity to work in television, I was truly the new kid on the block. I came to New York to work on national television, and wasn't just someone who fell off the turnip truck; I was about as sophisticated as a turnip. But I was also a sponge—not unlike a certain furry, red three-and-a-half-year-old—who absorbed and observed everything. I was working with some of the masters of the industry, and I paid close attention to everything they did. (And I'm still learning!)

"Elmo's World" is entirely made up of elements he's created. The set is a crayon drawing of his own making, he pounds away enthusiastically on his piano, he makes up his own lyrics daily, and he expresses his imaginative life through art. These elements of the set and the show are an expression of the sheer delight Elmo takes in learning. He loves his computer and his television because they help him answer his many questions. Elmo is as open-minded as most children his age are.

Elmo's concluding song—always the Jingle Bells tune—never feels repetitious to him because each time he sings it, he does so with new words to celebrate the knowledge he's gained. He may or may not have initiated that learning, but it is fueled by his insatiable desire to know more, it is fed by his joy of learning, and it is nurtured by a richly supportive environment. No wonder he bursts out into song at the end of each "Elmo's World" episode. Elmo's a lot like those preschoolers and elementary school kids you can see most days, running onto playgrounds or heading into classrooms, eyes bright with excitement about the possibilities that lay ahead of them.

BY PERFORMING ELMO for the last twenty years, I've naturally been drawn into the world of education, and I have a deep appreciation for what teachers do for our kids. I know that I was blessed with a number of wonderful teachers in my life, and the quality of Shannon's education is a reflection of the abilities of the faculty and staff at her school. The best teachers, like the best parents, have a tireless devotion to the well-being of children.

But even the most dedicated teachers can find it hard to carry out their mission in today's public school environment, particularly when faced with budget cuts. Because of my personal interests and my work in public television, every day I learn more about the politics of education.

In 2002, Elmo and I went to Washington, D.C. (he wore a suit and tie), to testify in front of Congress at the Education Appropriations Subcommittee, which was investigating the effects of eliminating funding for school arts programs. Even in affluent school districts, public schools face cost-cutting measures as they struggle to balance ballooning costs with shrinking budgets. With alarming frequency, programs in the visual arts and music—considered "electives"—are often the first items to be cut.

Elmo and I made an impassioned plea on behalf of all kids who benefit from these programs, particularly music. Though I wasn't really nervous, I was glad to be under the table—this was Congress, after all. "Elmo is here because he wants to make sure Elmo has music when he gets to school." The words came easily enough since I had been one of many kids for whom in-school and after-school arts programs were a lifeline. Playing trombone was some of the most fun

I had in school, though I can't say it was a pleasure for the folks who had to listen to me. No, I wasn't destined to blow the horn, but music kept me engaged and certainly livened up my school experience.

Music still is a big part of *Sesame Street*, and many professionals in the arts and education understand the benefits that kids can reap when they are exposed to this art form from an early age. *Sesame Street* is a great place to hear all sorts of music, and artists like Wynton Marsalis (a great supporter of music in the schools), Itzhak Perlman, Sheryl Crow, REM, Yo-Yo Ma, and many others, from opera singers to hip-hop stars and rockers, have all appeared on the show.

The lessons I learned in the world of theater and music have stayed with me to this day. I'd hate to think that shows like *Sesame Street* are the only places where kids can get a taste of the arts. I realize that most children in school-sponsored programs won't go on to have professional careers as artists, musicians, or puppeteers, but learning happens on many levels, and a basic foundation in the arts should be part of any well-rounded quality education.

It would be a shame for one kid to lose interest in school, perhaps even to the point of dropping out, as a result of budget cuts. Somewhere out there, there's a child—a first grader, a middle schooler, a junior in high school—whose growing passion for dance or painting or graphic design or music is what keeps her motivated to show up.

That day in Congress, a furry red monster helped to get the attention of our policy makers and urge them to think of the important role that art and music play in the education of a child.

MY PARENTS NEVER sat me down and had what I've come to refer to as "the talk." For a lot of my peers—and I know many performers whose harshest critics were their own families—the talk came just as they were entering the last year of high school. I can completely understand the parental impulse to steer a child in the right direction, but the artist in me cringes at the idea of words like "You know, you're never going to make any money doing this puppet [or acting/dancing/painting/photography] thing. It's nice that you have fun, but you need to go to college, you need to learn some skills to get a job in the real world."

Well, I started making money as a puppeteer when I was twelve. I had gigs on two local children's television shows while I was still in high school. I was earning more than I would have by delivering newspapers, mowing lawns, or babysitting, *and* I was having fun. I was also out there in the real world of adults and business, and if that's not learning, I don't know what is. For me, not going to college was the right choice, though that's certainly not the case for every young person.

We go to school to learn—from our instructors, from our books, from each other. And at some point, we begin to listen to another teacher: our dreams. We think about what could be, what might happen once we're all grown up, what we might be able to do with our budding talents or our latest interests.

Dreams are fragile things, but when they've been bolstered by the support of parents and teachers, and reinforced with early success, they can withstand the skeptics and take flight. When I was a kid, my dad and I spent a lot of time together building things, and I can't help but think of this metaphor: Kids are the architects of their own dreams. I know that I was.

That doesn't mean that children don't need an adult's help in making those dreams a reality. You already know what my parents did for me. But if you weren't there helping to build that solid foundation, don't come in with a wrecking ball later when you think the building is tilting too much. Maybe you were too busy when your child was learning how to draw. Maybe he wanted the building to tilt that way.

You can teach your children all the basics and then some, and they will turn right around and use their knowledge in wonderful, powerful ways you can't even imagine. That's the beauty of learning. But it can be hard to resist pulling on the reins and, at some point, steering kids away from what they want to learn to what you think they need to know to be successful. "Oh, no, he's just spending way too much time thinking about airplanes and not enough learning his math." "All she draws are pictures of houses and buildings, no people." Maybe he really will be a pilot; maybe she'll be an architect, or a famous artist. You just never know—but your child does.

I'm glad that Shannon shares my love of drawing, sculpting, and making things. I also know that I've learned from her along the way.

That point was driven home when I was asked to speak at her school for show-and-tell.

I couldn't help but flash back to my Russia report days as I sat in the classroom waiting my turn. Shannon's growing up now, and image is important to her, so when I walked up to the front of the room with Elmo, she came up with me. Smart kid. While I was talking, I kept hearing "No, Dad. Tell them about . . ." and a few other instructions to steer clear of anything too personal that might embarrass her. I learned a little bit about how Mr. Noodle must feel. That's okay. It was just another reminder that kids are teachers, too.

9

OPTIMISM

LHM'06

THE ELDERLY LADY had lost everything. In 2005, Hurricane Katrina took her home, her furniture, her food and clothing, all her possessions—including one of her most valued ones, her plush red Elmo. She was very sad that her "buddy," as she called him, had been lost. She had spoken to him daily, and now he was gone, too.

When Donna Chandler, the vice president of Global Outreach at Sesame Workshop, heard this story (the storm victim is the aunt of a reading specialist whom Donna has worked with), she immediately sent her a replacement. Eventually the woman's niece was able to visit her aunt, expecting to find an embittered and depressed old woman, still in shock over losing her home.

Instead, she found a smiling, vibrant lady who said, "Things are okay. My buddy's come back to visit me." She reached over and gave Elmo a squeeze, and he sang and danced the hokey pokey, as only Elmo can. Both women giggled like schoolgirls. The niece reached across the table to get Elmo to dance again, but her aunt suddenly grew serious. "Oh, no! You can't wear him out—his batteries only last so long. But he really makes me laugh and smile."

Elmo is a bundle of optimism, just like the children (both young and old) who love him. He's learning that life has its rough patches, but he lives in a world where he is supported by a caring group of friends and family (yes, that's a crayon drawing of his parents on the wall in "Elmo's World") who help him get through his days. And Elmo's frequent interactions with babies—those born optimists—lift his spirits and help him view the world as a place of hope and possibility.

I'm an optimist, too. When I hear about people like that Katrina victim, one of the thousands who have shown such resilience and who still manage to have a positive outlook, I truly do feel that everything will be okay. I volunteered to join a team of children's television performers to travel to the New Orleans area in the wake of the storm to entertain kids. I went down there with a heavy heart, but when I returned to New York, despite the physical devastation I'd seen, I felt hopeful and inspired by all the people I met on my travels.

The Corporation for Public Broadcasting (CPB), led by Senior Vice President of Educational Services Peggy O'Brien, arranged for our trip. The show *Between the Lions* tapes in Mississippi (it is produced in part by Mississippi Public Broadcasting), and its cast had already done a few local shows for displaced victims. *Lions* executive producer Judith Stoia and Peggy O'Brien created a minitour with stops in Louisiana (Baton Rouge and Lafayette) and Mississippi (Long Beach and Ocean Springs). They wanted to go to New Orleans, but this was mid-October, and authorities were limiting access to the most heavily damaged areas.

My *Sesame Street* castmates Maria (Sonia Manzano), Alan (Alan Muraoka), and Papa Bear (Joey Mazzarino), along with Leona from *Between the Lions* (Pam Arciero) and a walk-around Arthur character from the animated *Arthur* series, visited a host of schools during the four-day tour. The Sesame Workshop donated DVDs, Fisher-Price contributed Elmo toys, the organization First Book provided books, and the visit was a big success.

CPB continued to push for a New Orleans tour, and finally, on November 28, I joined my colleagues from the show—Emilio Delgado (who plays Luis), Alan Muraoka, and Lisa Buckley, as well as Pam Arciero and Carmen Osbahr. Freelance producer and director Lisa Simon, who had been to Sri Lanka following the tsunami to work on relief efforts there, coordinated our visit.

I really didn't know what to expect when I arrived at the airport and the bus took us into New Orleans, and as it turned out, I didn't have a lot of time to take it all in. We had a rehearsal scheduled for five-thirty that same day, and this was one show we all wanted to be prepared for. But in the end, it didn't matter how good the show was. We were there as much to comfort as to entertain.

We went to inner-city schools, where we performed in buildings with collapsed walls and boarded-up windows. Classes were being held there because those schools were in the *best* condition. Often the students were a mix of kids from three or four other schools, where combined faculty and staff made a heroic effort to establish some kind of normalcy in the lives of children who'd seen too much and lost too much. We did four shows a day, and we were grateful each time we got off the bus and entered another school. We could forget the destruction we saw on the street and focus instead on the hope inside those school buildings.

Amid all that devastation, there were reasons to be optimistic, particularly when we encountered adults and children who were determined to get through the crisis. At our very first stop, at Saint Louis Cathedral School (Cathedral Academy), the principal, Sister Mary Rose Bingham, did a warm-up act for us. Our audience was a group of first through third graders, and Sister Mary Rose danced for them and with them. She made a special effort to reach out to the kids who were less receptive, the ones who seemed particularly shell-shocked.

We took our lead from her and made it our mission to connect with as many kids as possible, often with a touch or a hug. As always, some children craved the contact while others hung back and watched from the sidelines, but this was different from any other live appearance. It was hard not to wonder if the reluctant children were holding back because of what they'd been through; at the same time, it seemed as if the kids who wanted to throw their arms around us were looking for extra reassurance and love after the trauma of the storm.

A number of children were especially difficult to reach, with their blank expressions and their empty gazes. Still, we persisted, working hard for every smile and laugh, forgetting the forty-five-minute structure we'd decided on and taking as much time as we needed to get through to the kids.

There were moments, though, when my optimism wavered. At one Head Start program, some of the kids were particularly unresponsive. We tried to make the show as interactive as possible, with sing-alongs and dancing, but the audience was quieter than most. Afterward, a teacher said to me, "They may not show it, but these kids really do appreciate this. In the best of times, they don't get a lot of attention—their lives have never been easy. They had problems before Katrina. Some of these kids are sleeping in abandoned buildings on concrete floors. Some are sleeping in cars."

We needed that reminder. The calm, structured moments these children spent in school were a stark contrast to the chaos in the rest of their lives, and now the chaos had been multiplied.

At another show. I asked a little girl of about six to name her favorite book. She smiled and said, "My favorite book is . . ." Her expression went blank, and she closed her eyes and sighed. "My favorite book *was* . . . " That change in tense said it all. I walked over to Lisa Simon, my head spinning, and said, "She lost everything."

Lisa told me about two little girls who were seated on folding chairs in the auditorium where we were performing. All the other children were sitting on the floor. Lisa had gently encouraged the girls to get up closer to the show. The pair shook their heads, and Lisa asked them why they didn't want to. The older of the two tugged at the skirt she was wearing and said, "We don't have any underwear."

Still, there were reasons to hope.

At one show at a shelter, we were out in front of the building unloading our puppets from the van. A boy of about ten or eleven was there on his own watching us. Suddenly he stepped forward and punched the Leona the Lion puppet. I was startled, as was everybody else. Instead of reprimanding him, though, Pam Arciero took him aside and talked with him. In the middle of the show, she had him up and puppeteering with her. I don't know where that sullen and angry young boy went, but he wasn't onstage. And he was nowhere to be seen after the show, when Pam asked the boy to help put Leona in her case. He held that puppet like he was cradling a baby, and instead of taking her straight to the case, he carried her around the room, showing him off to the youngest kids like a proud father.

When we went to perform for kids from the St. John the Baptist Head Start program, we could hear the excited buzz of our young audience before we even saw them, seated in the cafeteria. As we entered the kid-packed space, one voice rose above all the others. "Remember me? Remember me?" A lively young girl in braids and pink corduroy pants and a green Tulane sweatshirt stood in front of us, jumping in place and waving.

It took a second, but then we did remember. Just two days earlier, we had seen her at one of the shelters. By late November, most of the kids had been placed, and she was one of the last to remain. We'd spent a good bit of time with her, and we all commented later on how ashen her skin was, how dark crescent moons settled under her eyes, and how she mumbled every response. What a transformation! Now that she was in school and among her peers, she was an entirely different child.

It gave us hope to see these kids being kids again, and in their own way, they were setting an example for the adults around them. Their optimism was a much-needed reminder that life would keep going and that it would get better.

IN 1994, JUST a few years before I would travel to South Africa to audition puppeteers for *Takalani Sesame*, Nelson Mandela—a man who'd spent nearly three decades of his life in jail and became a symbol of resilience—was elected president of that country in its first truly free democratic election. I've already told you about *Takalani Sesame* and its courageous decision to include the HIV-positive character Kami. The other amazing thing about this trip was that it took place in 1999, not too long after apartheid had been dismantled and the country's black majority finally had a place at the table.

As an African American—and as the son of a proud black woman and man—I was deeply moved by the changes I saw. We spent most of our time in Johannesburg, where the emerging new reality was evident everywhere, from the vibrant green, black, and yellow banners of the African National Congress (banned for decades, but now with its candidate in the highest office), to signs in English, Afrikaans, Xhosa, Zulu, and a host of other languages proclaiming a new day. One of the many slogans I remember summed it up the best: *South Africa, Alive with Possibility.*

Our relationship with the South African production company mirrored what was going on in the rest of the country. Kwasuka-sukela (which, appropriately enough, means "once upon a time" in Zulu), was a partnership between a white-led media company in South Africa and a group of black filmmakers. Until this point in their careers, these black artists had had to work outside the mainstream of white-dominated South African media. Later I learned that many had used their skills for political purposes, documenting the abuses of race and privilege taking place throughout their country. Some of these people had been jailed for their activities, and every one of them considered him- or herself a political activist.

Starting any production from the ground up involves loads of decision making, but the issues we had to deal with in helping to plan *Takalani Sesame* were staggering. Which of the *eleven* official languages in the country should the characters speak? Should it be Xhosa, Zulu, Tsonga, Venda, or any of the others? Should the characters speak more than one? Do the puppet characters have an ethnicity?

In the U.S. version of *Sesame Street*, a monster is a monster and we don't think of them as having any kind of ethnic equivalent, but given South Africa's history and the population's makeup, ethnicity was extremely important. One of the first decisions the producers made was that Zuzu, the purple monster, would be a black South African. And to make a purple monster "black," we had to discuss what traits besides skin color would clearly identify someone in South Africa as black.

One of the most impressive people I've ever met in my life is the executive producer from Kwasukasukela, a woman named Seipati Bulane-Hopa, a black South African for whom English was her fourth language. Because of her background and ability to speak so many languages, she bridged the cultural divide that existed between the South African and American groups as well as within her own company. She was the one who led the discussion of blackness to the conclusion that Zuzu should have two different hairstyles. A lively debate about dreads, cornrows, twists, and Afros ensued.

My main task in going to South Africa was to train and select the puppeteers. I love this part of the work, even though it really hurts when I have to tell a performer that he or she hasn't been selected. I spent hour after intense hour in training these performers, and despite our language and cultural differences, a real bond formed. I cared deeply about each of the characters and wanted the right person to perform each one. Hundreds of puppeteers, an impressively diverse group that reflected the country's population, came from every part of South Africa to audition.

When it came time to choose the person to play the South African Elmo Neno, we narrowed the choice to four candidates who represented the broad spectrum of racial and ethnic groups in South Africa. Over time, it became clear who the best candidate was. Without a moment's thought about its possible implications, the all-black South African production company and I agreed that a white South African, Damian Berry, a young man who spoke no native languages besides his own Afrikaans, was the best fit. We all looked at each other and thought, *That's interesting.* Then we moved on to the next task on our list. We knew we'd hired the right person.

One day we traveled to a school outside of Johannesburg to perform. The city itself had impressed me; everything was so clean and orderly. But as we headed for the outskirts, I was reminded of many of the poorer urban neighborhoods in American big cities, and then I saw shantytowns unlike anything I'd ever seen except in photographs. Despite the poverty, though, no matter where we were, people waved and smiled. The entire black population seemed to be locked in permanent celebration mode. It seemed entirely fitting that the South African production was named *Takalani Sesame. Takalani* means "be happy" in the Venda language, and that spirit infused the country.

The countryside was starkly beautiful, with its reddish-orange soil and scrub trees. Eventually the regular road turned to a dusty track, and all along the way as we approached our destination, we saw young children ranging in age from what looked to be five to teens walking along the shoulder. They'd wave and trot after us for a few seconds. The school we were heading for was located on a farm, actually a large estate covering hundreds of miles, which employed the families of many of these children.

The estate was owned and operated by a very old and wealthy white South African family named Bailey whose wealth, we eventually learned, had partially been earned in the gold mining industry. Contrary to what we expected of a family with a background like that, the Baileys were a very progressive left-wing clan of activists who helped end apartheid. Jim Bailey, the patriarch, had a long history of activism and was a major supporter of the arts. He cofounded the influential *Drum* magazine in 1951, becoming one of the first South Africans to publish black writers. He'd even visited New York during the Harlem Renaissance, touring the area with the acclaimed poet Langston Hughes. This trip was proving to be full of surprises.

A number of black families lived on the hundreds of sprawling acres of the estate, call Leeuwenkloof Farm. It was still a working agricultural operation, but the primary school was the center of most of the activity. The residents sent their kids to the school, and all those children we'd seen walking along the road were students as well, many of them walking two hours each way to take advantage of the wonderful opportunity to receive a quality education.

None of the children had ever heard of or seen Elmo. Most had never seen a puppet before, so it took a long time for me to get the younger ones to interact with him. In a lot of ways, those kids were like timid cats. They'd sit back on their haunches, looking at Elmo, and then they'd come forward slightly to rest on all fours to get a closer look. As soon as I moved Elmo, they retreated. Sometimes I would take Elmo off, set him aside, and just talk with the kids as myself. Once they got used to me, I'd put Elmo back on and he'd quietly talk to them. I spent a lot of time on my knees coaxing these kids to move in closer. Eventually I figured out that if I just set Elmo down and left him lying there, their curiosity would get the better of them and they'd come to me. We didn't speak the same language or have a translator, but Elmo's magic worked just the same. By the end of the visit, the kids were laughing and singing, and Elmo got his usual share of hugs and kisses and distributed an equal number, as well.

On so many levels, this experience had a profound impact on me. It was only after I'd returned to the States that I could really take stock of all that had happened and what it meant to me as a performer and as a person. Obviously, it had been thrilling to be in South Africa. Anytime I travel to a new place, I'm energized, but this was different. Something about this groundbreaking experience snuck up on me after I came home.

I realized the trip had taken me back to the days when I was working with Stu Kerr, doing shows in the Baltimore area. At the conclusion of the performance, he'd have me come out from behind the puppet stage and curtain to take a bow. I'd step out there and I'd hear a few oohs and ahhs of surprise. People had no idea I was black, and that was cool. But when the black audience members saw it was *me* doing these things, they clapped a little bit harder and their loud shouts of "Great show!" grew more heartfelt and genuine.

I was not and am not a pioneer in any way, but what the people at Kwasukasukela were doing, and what the people of South Africa were doing, was truly revolutionary. The fact that *Takalani Sesame* got off the ground at the same time that the new South Africa was taking shape made me especially proud.

On another hopeful note, despite the controversy in the U.S. about *Takalani Sesame* introducing the HIV-positive character Kami (and the fears that the American *Sesame Street* might do the same), UNICEF appointed Kami a global Champion for Children in November of 2003. Even if one mind closes, thousands of others are opened. By the way, the name "Kami" is derived from a Tswana word for "acceptance."

CHILDREN ARE ALL about promise and new beginnings, about moving forward and not backward. Kids in places like New Orleans and Johannesburg are like kids everywhere—they represent the possibilities in life. When we feel stuck or just down, it's easy to dwell on what was and what could have been, but children remind us that we don't grow and that things don't get better unless we keep looking ahead.

As a teenager, I caught a glimpse of my own future that day I saw Kermit Love on TV, in his workshop. A few years later, I myself was the subject of a "career day" feature on the show *Big Blue Marble*. They wanted to showcase me, a young puppeteer, working on the set of *Caboose*. The cameras filmed me and my father, who dropped me off at the train station in Baltimore, where I would commute to New York City. They showed Kermit teaching me how to build puppets and then me building puppets at home in Turner's Station and, finally, doing a live performance in front of a group that became one of my favorite audiences—the students at the Battle Monument School. (I was so proud to be showcased in this way—but, I admit, I was really flattered by the fact that they'd asked me to shave my mustache for the segment . . . I finally looked old enough to shave!)

Somewhere out there, I bet some kid was watching me, optimistic and excited about the future, dreaming about the possibilities that life held, wondering if there was such a thing as a happy ending.

"And they all lived happily ever after," right? Well, my own fairy tale is far from over because I'm still living it. When I come home from work each day, I'm usually pretty exhausted, but in a good way. I honestly feel like I just spent the day with a very active, joyful, and wildly optimistic three-and-a-half-year-old, one who always wants to know more and, most of all, to *be* more.

Elmo may not use a lot of big words, and he may not be very tall, but day after day, he's bursting with a message of hope and is full of enthusiasm for life. Like children all over the globe, he teaches us that we can always reach a little higher, jump a little farther, do a little better. What would happen if we all lived our lives that way? Maybe it would mean a happy ending.

That's Elmo's world. It can be our world, too.

ACKNOWLEDGMENTS

I **AM SO GRATEFUL** for the love and support my family has given me—Mom and Dad, Shannon, George, Ne-Ne, Pam, Genia, and especially Michel.

I thank Becky Cabaza, who really pulled everything together and made this a wonderful book.

I would also like to graciously thank Gary Brozek for his time and the endless hours spent on the phone trying to make sense of everything.

Thank you to Elizabeth Payne for her creative contribution to *My Life as a Furry Red Monster*.

To Gary Knell, Mel Ming, and all my friends at Sesame Workshop, "YOU'RE THE BEST!"

To Ron Kreidman, my lawyer and good friend, who is always there. Thank you.

To Jim Wiseman and Geanie Bond, my spiritual advisers, if only I listened to them.

Thanks to Peter Steinberg for seeing that there was a book here.

To Trish Medved, thank you for educating me on how a book should be done. And to the folks at Broadway Books, thanks for everything you have done to make this book happen.

Louis Mitchell, you're a godsend.

Coop, you know what you mean to me.

To Jim Martin, you have always been there to help me out. You will always be a brother of mine.

Neil Friedman, thank you for being such a good friend to this little red monster and this tall black man.

Kimi Sokol, you continue to be the best personal assistant any crazy man could ask for (Brad, you can have her back one of these days).

Ellen Lewis, I am so appreciative of your undying support and your willingness always to go above and beyond for me.

To my mentors, Stu Kerr, Kermit Love, Bob Keeshan, Jim Henson, Joan Ganz Cooney, and Caroll Spinney, thank you for believing in me.

AND ELMO LOVES ALL OF YOU FOR BEING THERE FOR KEVIN

ABOUT THE AUTHOR

KEVIN CLASH began making his own puppets and performing for live audiences when he was a boy. He turned his childhood obsession into a professional passion, forging a career in television and making an indelible mark on children's imaginations. Kevin has been with *Sesame Street* for twenty-six years and is coexecutive producer of "Elmo's World." He has won three Emmy Awards for Outstanding Performer in a Children's Series and five for his work as coexecutive producer of an Outstanding Pre-School Children's Series. He has a daughter, Shannon, and lives in New York City.